C000006210

PARLIAMENT SQUARE

James Fritz

Royal Exchange Theatre, Manchester
18–28 October 2017

Bush Theatre, London
30 November 2017–6 January 2018

The first performance of *Parliament Square* was at the
Royal Exchange Theatre on 18 October 2017

Parliament Square

by James Fritz

CAST

VOICE/JO	Lois Chimimba
KAT	Esther Smith
TOMMY	Damola Adelaja
DOCTOR/ANNOUNCER/ FRIEND/TAXI DRIVER	Jamie Zubairi
PHYSIO/COLLEAGUE/ TICKET WOMAN/FRIEND	Kelly Hotten
MUM	Joanne Howarth
CATHERINE	Seraphina Beh

CREATIVE TEAM

DIRECTOR	Jude Christian
DESIGNER	Fly Davis
LIGHTING DESIGNER	Jack Knowles
SOUND DESIGNERS	Ben & Max Ringham
MOVEMENT DIRECTOR	Jennifer Jackson
ASSISTANT DIRECTOR	Amy Hailwood
CASTING DIRECTORS	Jerry Knight-Smith CDG & Vicky Richardson
STAGE MANAGER	Sophie Tetlow
DEPUTY STAGE MANAGER	Hannah Phillips

With thanks to Bethany Wells

The development of *Parliament Square* has been supported by the Banff Centre Playwrights Lab which, in partnership with Bruntwood, offered James Fritz a residency as a winner of a Judges Award at the 2015 Bruntwood Prize for Playwriting. The Banff Centre Playwrights Lab offers Canadian and international playwrights an inspiring environment to work on their plays while surrounded by performing artists from across the country and around the world.

Cast

LOIS CHIMIMBA (Voice/Jo) is making her first appearance for the Royal Exchange Theatre and Bush Theatre. Other theatre credits include: *Common* (National Theatre); *Peter Pan* (National Theatre/Bristol Old Vic); *Diary of a Mad Man* (Traverse/Gate); *Wonder.land* (National Theatre/Manchester International Theatre); *Pitcairn* (Out of Joint/ Shakespeare's Globe/Chichester); *Nightingale and Chase* (Stonecrabs). Television credits include: *Trust Me*, *Radges*, *Fried*, *Holby City*. Radio credits include: *Homefront*.

ESTHER SMITH (Kat) is making her first appearance at the Bush Theatre. She has previously appeared at the Royal Exchange Theatre in *The Author*. Other theatre credits include: *Harry Potter and the Cursed Child* (Palace; original cast member); *NSFW* (Royal Court); *The Honeyman* (Derby Live); *Carrot* (Theatre503/Latitude Festival); *Many Moons* (Theatre503); *Limbs (Present Tense)* (nabokov); *The Author* (Royal Court/international tour); *Romeo and Juliet* (The Chocolate Factory); *This Child* (Southwark Playhouse). Television credits include: *Uncle* (series regular), *Cuckoo* (series regular), *Ballot Monkeys*, *Black Mirror*, *Cockroaches*, *Flack*, *The Midnight Beast*, *The Smoke*, *Holby City*, *Skins Redux: Rise*, *Deadbeats*, *Misfits*, *Material Girl*, *Elephant* (co-wrote & Bafta nominated).

DAMOLA ADELAJA (Tommy) is making his first appearance at the Bush Theatre. He has previously appeared at the Royal Exchange Theatre in *A Raisin in the Sun*. Other theatre credits include: *Our Country's Good* (St James/tour); *Fixer* (Ovalhouse); *A Drop to Drink* (Soho); *Slave* (Lowry); *Junun Dementia* (GBS Theatre); *Ruined* (Almeida); *The Crossing* (Hall For Cornwall/Theatre503). Television credits include: *Berlin Station*, *EastEnders* and *Doctors*. Film credits include: *The Huntsman*, *The Circus*, *Rag Tag*.

JAMIE ZUBAIRI (Doctor/Announcer/Friend/ Taxi Driver) is making his first appearance for the Royal Exchange Theatre and Bush Theatre. Other theatre credits include: *Miss Meena and the Masala Queens* (Watford Palace); *The Letter* (Wyndham's); *Other People's Shoes* (Barbican Plymouth); *Burmese Days* (Aya Theatre/53e53 New York); *Wolf* (Authentic Artist Collective, Edinburgh); *Cheese* (FanShen); *A Doll's House* (Theatre of Europe); *Counted?* (LookLeft LookRight); *Dogs* (Ovalhouse/Yellow Earth). Television credits include: *Silent Witness, Holby City, Cuckoo, Grange Hill, Cucumber*. Film credits include: *Tides* (actor & co-writer), *Project Alcatraz*. Radio credits include: *Inspector Chen Mysteries* (series regular), *Lek & Mrs Miller*. Theatre writing credits include: *Unbroken Line, Expectations* (Ovalhouse).

KELLY HOTTEN (Physio/Colleague/Ticket Woman/Friend) trained at Drama Centre London. She is making her first appearance for the Bush Theatre. She has previously appeared at the Royal Exchange Theatre in *Our Town, The Night Watch, A Doll's House* and *As You Like It*. Other theatre credits include: *Inkheart* (HOME); *The 39 Steps* (Criterion, West End); *Dial M for Murder* (UK tour, Fiery Angel); *Perfect Match* (Watford Palace); *Chavs* (Lyric Hammersmith); *An Inspector Calls* (UK tour, PW); *The Duchess of Malfi, In Bed with Messalina, Edward II* (Eyestrings); *Macbeth* (Cheek by Jowl); *Theatre Café* (Company of Angels/Unicorn); *Hades* (Theatre503); *Playlist* (Arcola); *The Girl, The Oil Pipe and The Murder in the Forum* (Tara Arts); *Virgins* (Vienna's English Theatre). Television credits include: *Doctors, WPC 56*.

JOANNE HOWARTH (Mum) is making her first appearance for the Bush Theatre. She has previously appeared at the Royal Exchange Theatre in *You Can't Take It With You*. Other theatre credits include: *Nell Gwynn* (ETT/Shakespeare's Globe); *King Lear* (Old Vic); *Much Ado About Nothing* (Shakespeare's Globe/tour); *Goodnight Mr Tom* (West End/tour); *I Am a Camera* (Southwark Playhouse); *Bingo* (Chichester/ Young Vic); *The Comedy of Errors, Twelfth Night, Faust, The Alchemist, The Virtuoso, 'Tis Pity She's a Whore* (RSC); *Hallelujah* (Theatre503); *Shadowmouth* (Sheffield Crucible); *After the Dance* (OSC); *The Firework Maker's Daughter* (Told by an Idiot); *The Pull of Negative Gravity* (Traverse/Off Broadway); *Singer* (Tricycle); *Present Laughter* (Bath tour); *Who Goes There?* (Dreamthinkspeak); *East is East* (Leicester Haymarket); *Romeo and Juliet* (Wolsey Ipswich). Film and television credits: *Making Noise Quietly, Innocents, Spooks, Wallander, EastEnders, Waking the Dead, Doctors, Grange Hill*.

SERAPHINA BEH (Catherine) is making her first appearance for the Royal Exchange Theatre. She has previously appeared at the Bush Theatre in *Black Attack*. Other theatre credits include: *Pigeon English*, *Romeo and Juliet*, *DNA* (National Youth Theatre); *Cosmic Jives* (Albany); *My Beautiful City* (Arcola); *Jack and the Beanstalk* (Lyric Hammersmith); *Ondisting*, *Romeo & Juliet Et Al*, *Skeen* (Ovalhouse). Television credits include: *EastEnders*, *Casualty*, *Game Face*, *Live at the Electric*.

Creative Team

JAMES FRITZ (Writer) James's first full-length play, *Four Minutes Twelve Seconds*, was runner-up of the Soho Theatre's 2013 Verity Bargate Award. It premiered at Hampstead Theatre Downstairs in 2014 and was nominated for an Olivier Award for Outstanding Achievement in an Affiliate Theatre before transferring to Trafalgar Studios in 2015. It then won him the 'Most Promising Playwright' Prize at the Critics' Circle Theatre Awards 2015. His other plays include *Ross & Rachel* ('a virtuosic piece of writing' *Time Out*) which opened to critical acclaim at the Edinburgh Festival Fringe 2015 before playing off-Broadway and touring the UK twice, *Parliament Square*, which won a Bruntwood Prize in 2015 and *The Fall* which he wrote for the National Youth Theatre's 60th anniversary season in 2016. In 2017 his radio play *Comment Is Free* won both the Imison and the Tinniswood Awards at the BBC Audio Drama Awards, which is the first time that a single writer has won both awards the same year.

JUDE CHRISTIAN (Director) As a director, theatre credits include: *Bodies, Lela & Co.* (Royal Court); *The Path* (HighTide Festival); *Split/Mixed* (Summerhall); *Blue* (RWCMD/Gate); *How Do You Eat an Elephant? Bwyta Eliffant, Sut Mae Gwneud Hynny Dwedwch?* (Aberystwyth Arts Centre/tour); *Happy, The Mushroom* (Pentabus); *Punk Rock, Last Easter* (RADA); *I'd Rather Goya Robbed Me of My Sleep Than Some Other Arsehole* (Gate); *Balansera* (Remix Gold, Poole Lighthouse); *Sonata Movements* (Concert Theatre, Blue Elephant); *My Romantic History* (English Theatre Berlin). Co-director credits include: *Jack and the Beanstalk* (Lyric Hammersmith). As an associate director, her credits include: *The Darkest Corners* (RashDash/Transform Festival); *The Seagull, Aladdin, Shopping and Fucking* (Lyric Hammersmith); *Carmen Disruption* (Almeida). Opera credits include: *Hidden in Plain Sight* (Académie du Festival d'Aix-en-Provence, in association with Opera Lab Berlin) and *@alculated To Death* (Tête à Tête opera festival, White Lab, Central St Martins).

FLY DAVIS (Designer) Previous designs for the Royal Exchange Theatre include: *Our Town, How My Light Is Spent* (also Sherman Theatre and Theatre by the Lake), *A Streetcar Named Desire, Scuttlers, Hunger for Trade* and *Nothing*. Previous designs for the Bush Theatre include: Russell Kane's *The Great British Country Fête Musical* (also UK tour). Other design credits include: *The Comedy of Errors, I Want My Hat Back, The Beginning* (National Theatre; Olivier nominated); *A Tale of Two Cities, Oliver Twist* (Regent's Park Open Air Theatre); *Caroline, or Change* (Chichester Festival Theatre); *Othello* (Shakespeare's Globe); *A Winter's Tale* (Lyceum); *Trade, Barbarians* (Olivier nominated); *Turning a Little Further, A Streetcar Named Desire* (Young Vic); *The Remains of Maisie Duggan* (Abbey, Dublin); *Unreachable* (Royal Court, costume designer);

Contractions (Sheffield Crucible); *The Glass Menagerie* (Headlong/West Yorkshire Playhouse/Liverpool Playhouse/Richmond); *Opera for the Unknown Woman* (Fuel UK tour); *The Crocodile* (Manchester International Festival/Invisible Dot); *James and the Giant Peach* (West Yorkshire Playhouse); *I'd Rather Goya Robbed Me of My Sleep Than Some Other Arsehole, Image of an Unknown Young Woman* (Gate); *Primetime, Pigeons, Collaboration* (Royal Court); *Eye of a Needle, Superior Donuts* (Southwark Playhouse); *The Dissidents* (Tricycle); *Nick Mohammed's Dracula Mr Swallow The Musical!* (Soho/Invisible Dot); *Woyzeck* (Omnibus); *What the Animals Say* (Greyscale UK tour); *The Invisible Dot's Big Birthday Bash* (Hammersmith Apollo); *Love is Easy* (McFly music video). Awards: Off West End Award Best Set Design, Best Production for *Image of an Unknown Young Woman* (Gate).

JACK KNOWLES (Lighting Designer) Jack has previously worked at the Royal Exchange on *Our Town, Twelfth Night, A Streetcar Named Desire, Wit, The Skriker* (also Manchester International Festival), *There Has Possibly Been an Incident* and at the Bush Theatre on *Moth* (also HighTide). Other theatre credits include: *Committee* (Donmar Warehouse); *Barber Shop Chronicles, Cleansed* (National Theatre); *Caroline, or Change* (Chichester); *Junkyard, Pygmalion* (Headlong); *Winter Solstice* (Orange Tree); *They Drink It In The Congo, Boy, Carmen Disruption, Game* (Almeida); *Dan and Phil: The Amazing Tour Is Not On Fire* (world tour); *Watership Down* (Watermill); *Kenny Morgan* (Arcola); *The Massive Tragedy of Madame Bovary!* (Liverpool Everyman/ Peepolykus); *The Haunting of Hill House* (Liverpool Playhouse); *Phaedra* (Enniskillen International Beckett Festival); *Blink* (Traverse/Soho/ international tour); *In a Pickle* (RSC/Oily Cart); *Ring-A-Ding-Ding* (Unicorn/New Victory Theater, New York/Oily Cart); *Land of Lights, Light Show, There Was an Old Woman, The Bounce, Mr & Mrs Moon* (Oily Cart). His work with Katie Mitchell includes: *4.48 Psychosis, Reisende Auf Einem Bein, Happy Days* (Schauspielhaus, Hamburg); *The Forbidden Zone* (Salzburg Festival/Schaubühne, Berlin/Barbican); *2071* (Royal Court); *A Sorrow Beyond Dreams* (Vienna Burgtheater); *Lungs, Yellow Wallpaper* (Schaubühne, Berlin); *Say It With Flowers* (Hampstead); *Night Train* (Schauspiel, Köln/Avignon Festival/Theatertreffen).

BEN & MAX RINGHAM (Sound Designers) Previous work for the Royal Exchange Theatre includes: *Our Town, Persuasion, The Mighty Walzer*. This is their first production at the Bush Theatre. Other recent theatre includes: *The Pitchfork Disney* (Shoreditch Town Hall); *Lunch & The Bow of Ulysses, Doctor Faustus, The Maids* (Trafalgar Studios); *The Dresser* (Duke of York's); *After Miss Julie* (Theatre Royal Bath); *Deathtrap* (Salisbury Playhouse); *The Government Inspector* (Birmingham Rep); *Raz* (Assembly Theatre/Riverside Studios); *Queen Anne* (RSC); *Ben Hur, A Wolf in Snakeskin Shoes, Multitudes* (Tricycle); *La Musica, Ah, Wilderness!* (Young Vic); *The Mentalists* (Wyndham's); *We Want You To Watch* (National Theatre Temporary Space); *The Ruling Class, Richard III*

(Trafalgar Transformed); *The Walworth Farce* (Olympia, Dublin); *2071, Adler and Gibb* (Royal Court); *Minetti* (Edinburgh International Festival); *Dawn French* (UK tour); *Fiction* (UK tour); *Blithe Spirit* (Gielgud/US tour); *Boeing Boeing* (Sheffield Crucible); *I Can't Sing* (London Palladium) and *The Full Monty* (Sheffield/Noël Coward). Ben and Max are associate artists with the Shunt collective and two-thirds of the band Superthriller. In 2013 they designed 'Papa Sangre II' a sound-based IOS game for digital arts company Somethin' Else. They are also co-creators of the immersive theatre company Wiretapper. Awards: Off West End Award Best Sound Designer winner 2014 (Ring, BAC); IMGA Excellence in Sound Design Award winner 2014 (Papa Sangre II); Best Sound Design Olivier Award nomination 2012 (*The Ladykillers*); Best Sound Design Olivier Award nomination 2009 (Piaf); Best Overall Achievement in an Affiliate Theatre Olivier Award winner (as part of the creative team) 2009 (*The Pride*).

JENNIFER JACKSON (Movement Director) trained at East 15 and is a movement director and actor. Previous movement direction credits for the Royal Exchange Theatre include: *Our Town*. Other theatre credits include: *The Mountaintop* (Young Vic); *Black Mountain, How To Be A Kid, Out of Love* (Paines Plough Roundabout); *Death of a Salesman* (Royal & Derngate); *The Ugly One* (Park 90); *Phone Home* (Shoreditch Town Hall/BAC); *Why the Whales Came* (Southbank Centre); *Wuthering Heights* (workshop – Royal Exchange Theatre); *Stone Face, Silent Planet* (Finborough); *Debris* (Southwark Playhouse/OpenWorks); *Macbeth* (Passion in Practice/Sam Wanamaker Playhouse); *Pericles* (Berwaldhallen); *Subterranean Sepoys* (New Diorama); *The Future* (The Yard); *Other (Please Specify), Atoms* (Company Three); *Takeover 2017* (Tricycle). Assistant movement direction credits include: *Lungs, The Initiate, My Teacher's a Troll* (Paines Plough Roundabout 2014 – Fringe First Winners). Jennifer is an associate artist with OpenWorks Theatre, Upstart Theatre, and a member of Tangled Feet. As a performer Jennifer has worked with the NT, NT Studio, BAC, Bath Theatre Royal, Royal & Derngate Theatre (Argus Angel winner at the Brighton Festival), Sam Wanamaker Playhouse, Theatre503, Arcola, OpenWorks Theatre, Derby Theatre, The Yard, Harold Pinter Theatre (West End), Southwark Playhouse, Bervaldhallen (Stockholm), Lucas Theatre (Savannah, USA), Pearl Theatre (New York).

AMY HAILWOOD (Assistant Director) As a director, theatre credits include: *Come Closer: Memories of Partition* (Royal Exchange Theatre); *Joy Unspeakable* (Octagon, Bolton); *Faraway, So Close* (The Old Fire Station, Oxford). Amy is a member of the Open Exchange Network, the Royal Exchange's network dedicated to developing emerging artists and was the Observer Director on *A Streetcar Named Desire* at the Royal Exchange in 2016.

Manchester's Royal Exchange Theatre Company transforms the way people see theatre, each other and the world around them.

Our historic building, once the world's biggest cotton exchange, was taken over by artists in 1976. Today it is an award-winning cultural charity that produces new theatre in-the-round, in communities, on the road and online.

Exchange remains at the heart of everything we make and do. Now our currency is brand new drama and reinvigorated classics, the boldest artists and a company of highly skilled makers – all brought together to trade ideas and experiences with the people of Greater Manchester (and beyond).

The Exchange's unique auditorium is powerfully democratic, a space where audiences and performers meet as equals, entering and exiting through the same doors. It is the inspiration for all we do; inviting everyone to understand the past, engage in today's big questions, collectively imagine a better future and lose themselves in the moment of a great night out.

Autumn Winter 2017/18 is one of the biggest and most exciting seasons ever with four World Premieres, including two Bruntwood Prize Winners. Following *Parliament Square*, it continues with *Jubilee* – a brand new stage adaptation of Derek Jarman's film, by Chris Goode, *Guys and Dolls* in a co-production with Talawa Theatre, *The Almighty Sometimes* by Kendall Feaver, and *Black Men Walking* by Testament in a co-production with Eclipse Theatre Company.

Find out more at **royalexchange.co.uk**

 instagram.com/rxtheatre

 facebook/rxtheatre

 youtube.com/royalexchange.co.uk

Box Office **0161 833 0933**

 **AGMA** ASSOCIATION OF GREATER MANCHESTER AUTHORITIES

 MANCHESTER CITY COUNCIL

 LOTTERY FUNDED | Supported using public funding by ARTS COUNCIL ENGLAND

Registered Charity Number 255424

the bruntwood
prize for playwriting 2017

In partnership with the **Royal Exchange Theatre**

'It's not an exaggeration to say that winning a Bruntwood Judges Prize changed my life. It gave me the time, money and – crucially – support both to develop my play and to push my writing to new places. Winning the prize is nice – but it's what comes after, that proves what an incredible opportunity it is.'

James Fritz
2015 Judges Award winner

The Bruntwood Prize for Playwriting is Europe's biggest playwriting prize, awarding a total fund of £40,000 and development opportunities to UK based playwrights.

Since its inception in 2005, writers such as Duncan MacMillan, Anna Jordan, Phil Porter and Vivienne Franzmann have gone on to see their Bruntwood Prize-winning plays produced internationally.

If you are interested in playwriting, check out the wealth of resources on our website **writeaplay.co.uk**. Get tips and video tutorials from some of the country's leading theatre-makers and find out more on how to develop your own writing.

The Bruntwood Prize for Playwriting awards ceremony will be live streamed on **writeaplay.co.uk** from **4pm** on **Monday 13 November.**

ROYAL EXCHANGE THEATRE STAFF

CREATIVE LEARNING AND ENGAGEMENT
Director of Creative Learning Inga Hirst
Creative Learning and Engagement Interim Manager Chris Wright
Adults Programme Leader Andy Barry
Young People's Programme Leader Matt Hassall
Schools Programme Leader Chelsea Morgan
Youth Engagement Programme Leader (Outreach) Parvez Qadir
Community Programme Leader Tracie Daly
Administrator Emma Wallace

DEVELOPMENT
Development Director Val Young
Senior Development Manager Gina Fletcher
Individual Giving Manager Becky Rosenthal
Corporate Development Manager Christina Georgiou
Development Executive Holli Leah
Membership Manager Jessica Hilton

DIRECTORATE
Executive Director Mark Dobson
Artistic Director Sarah Frankcom
Associate Artistic Directors Amit Sharma, Matthew Xia
Associate Artists Amanda Dalton, Rash Dash, Chris Goode, Imogen Knight, Maxine Peake, Benji Reid, Chris Thorpe, Don Warrington
Assistant to the Artistic Directorate & Executive Director Michelle Hickman
Birkbeck Trainee Director Atri Banerjee

ELDERS COMPANY
Alan Maguire, Amina Latimer, Anne Tober, Anthony Joyce, Brenda Hickey, Charles McDermott, Christine Connor, Christopher Littler, David Weston, Donald McGregor, Doreen Robinson, Dudley Newell, Estelle Longmore, Glyn Treharne, Gordon Emerson, Graham Gillis, Jacquie Long, Janice Bonner, Jean Wood, Judith Wood, Kenneth Walker, Liz Aniteye, Marianne Downes, Maureen Stirpe, Michael Williams, Monica Farry, Pauline Sergeant, Pete Shotton, Peter Jones, Philip Haynes, Sandy Parkinson, Shelia Colman, Steve Stubbs, Tony Cocker, Val Collier

FINANCE & ADMINISTRATION
Director of Finance & Administration Barry James
HR Manager (Maternity Cover) Sara Spencer
Administrator Melissa Brakel
Finance Manager Sue Jones
Orders & Purchase Ledger Clerk Jennifer Ellis
Payroll Clerk Carl Robson
Finance Administrator Elizabeth Coupe

GREEN ROOM
Supervisor Yvonne Stott
Assistant Anne Dardis

MARKETING
Director of Marketing & Communications (Maternity Cover) Laura Arends
Head of Marketing Vanessa Walters
Communications Manager Paula Rabbitt
Marketing Officer – Groups, Education & Development Eleanor Higgins
Marketing Officer – Digital and Systems Vicky Wormald
Marketing Officer Anneka Morley
Digital Marketing Officer Ashley McKay
Marketing Assistant Justina Aina
Box Office Manager Sue Partington

Box Office Assistants William Barnett, Jon Brennan, Lindsay Burke, Tracey Fleet, Dan Glynn, Zoe Nicholas, Christine Simpson, Eleanor Walk

OPERATIONS
Operations Director Jo Topping
Visitor Experience Manager Lynne Yates
Deputy Visitor Experience Manager Stuart Galligan
Head of Facilities David Mitchell
Maintenance Technician Carl Johnson
IT Manager Ean Burgon
IT Support & Network Technician John Barlow
Volunteer Coordinator Kate Hardy
Deputy Retail Manager Gail Owen
Shop Assistants Elisa Robinson, Clare Sidebotham, Amber Samuels, Emily Tilzey, Jessica Sharp
Duty Managers Jill Bridgeman, Helen Coyne, Rachel Davies
Head Ushers Tracey Fleet, Heather Madden, Stuart Shaw
Security Liam Ainsworth, Liam Carty, Dave Hughes, Mike Seal
Stage Door Thomas Flaherty
Ushers Tom Banks, Georgie Brown, Helen Brown, Natasha Bybik, Elizabeth Callan, Liam Carty, Emily Chadwick, Richard Challinor, Alicia Cole, Elizabeth Coupe, Chris Dance, Anna Davenport, Cliona Donohue, Luther Edmead, Harry Egan, Amy Claire Evans, Paul Evans, Neil Fenton, Beth Galligan, Wesley Harding, Connie Hartley, Jennifer Hulman, Dan Lizar, Ben Lucas, Heather Madden, Sue McGonnell, Tony O'Driscoll, Elle Pemberton Steer, Alice Proctor, John Roy, Stuart Shaw, Vincent Tuohy, Edward (Ted) Walker, Judith Wood, Mahdi Zadeh

Cleaning Contractors
Head Cleaner Lillian Williams
Cleaners Gillian Bradshaw, Susan Burroughs, Elaine Connolly, Valarie Daffern, Jackie Farnell, Ahab Mohamed, Maryam Murmin, Daniel Thompson, Hussein Fatima Yassin

PRODUCTION
Head of Production Simon Curtis
Props Buyer Kim Ford
Production Coordinator Greg Skipworth
Driver John Fisher
Head of Technical Richard Delight
Head of Sound Sorcha Williams
Senior Sound Technicians Sam Leahy, Matt Sims
Sound Technician Matthew Masson
Head of Lighting Mark Distin-Webster
Senior Lighting Technicians Alex Dixon, Matthew Lever
Lighting Technician Louise Anderson
Technical Stage Manager Andy Roberts
Stage Technicians Simon Wild, Luke Murray
Head of Props and Settings Neil Gidley
Deputy Head of Props and Settings Andy Bubble
Workshop Supervisor Carl Heston
Senior Scenic Artist Phil Costello
Prop Makers Ben Cook, Stuart Mitchell, Sarah Worrall
Head of Wardrobe Nikki Meredith
Deputy Head of Wardrobe Tracy Dunk
Studio Wardrobe Supervisor Felicia Jagne
Tailor & Gents Cutter Rose Calderbank
Cutters Jennifer Adgey, Rachel Bailey
Hair and Make-up Supervisor Jo Shepstone
Costume Hire Manager Ludmila Krzak

With help from the volunteer team

PROGRAMME

Senior Producer
Ric Watts
Head of Casting & Associate Director
Jerry Knight-Smith CDG
Company Manager
Lee Gower-Drinkwater
New Writing Associate
Suzanne Bell
Producer Amy Clewes
Literary & Talent Development Administrator
Grace Ng-Ralph
Bruntwood Prize Coordinator
Chloe Smith
Assistant Producer
Max Emmerson

THE RIVALS BAR & RESTAURANT
Adam Abreu, Mark Beattie, Victoria Bowen, Leah Curran, Nick Edmead, Anna Fysh, Jose Garcia, Emma Gold, Rupert Hill, Sarah Hope, Tom Johnson, James Langrish, Malgorzata Langrish, Joseph Lester, Robin Lyons, Simon Mayne, Elle Pemberton, Helen Thomason, Damian Traczyk, Jake Tysome, Christopher Wilson

VOLUNTEERS
Sally Almond, Diane Amans, Anne Barnaby, Joan Beverly, Christine Brown, Nim Burgen, Noreen Burns, Pamela Burrow, Jim Capewell, Eileen Carleton, Claire Chatterton, Geoffrey Clifton, Norma Code, Joan Cowlishaw, Pat Cross,Salle Dare, Pat Dexter, Terry Donnelly, Beverley Dowling, Gill Edmondson, Maggie Evans, Claire Fern, Mary Findlay, Mildred Finney, Doreen Firth, Anne Fitzpatrick, Barbara Frankl, McGirr Georgia, Irene Gibbons, Norman Goodman, Irene Gray, Sue Hall Smith, Kate Sharples, Sylvia Hampton, Carolyn Harrison, Margaret Hatton, Enid Head, Margaret Higson, Grace Jackson, Julia Jessup, Jean Johnson, Pat Jones, Liz Kenny, Judith Khoudi, Debrah Lamb, Ann Laza, Jean Lea, Sheila Lorca, Stella Lowe, Sheila Lowe, Lillian Mills, Helen

Mitchell, Hilary Murray, John Pearsall, Robert Pegrum, Adrian Percival, Sally Phelan, Hilary M Poole, Maggie Radcliffe, Leila Raulfi, Ruth Salisbury, Rachael Seymour, Carole Shinkfield, Elwira Slama, Isobel Smith, Anne Smith, Alison Squire, Carol Street, Clare Stuart, Sheila Taylor, Josephine Taylor, Tzanka Tcherneva Illeva, Alison Thaw, Lis Todd-Jones, Angie Took, Eileen Tunbridge, Jane Unsworth, Pauline Walsh, Derek Waterhouse, Tonia Williams, Ann Winter, Elizabeth Wolstencroft, E G Young, Edna George, Joseph Kelly, Jamal Alamien, Henrietta Fusi, Abas Elijanabi, Astra Purvina, Ayla Huseyinoglu, Amanda Blake, Jane Costin, Mark Dickenson, Steven Kelly, Leah Gray Scaife, Terence Robinson, Bethany Raffles, Lauren Young, Juliet Morris, Shiela Aris, Harry Ranson, Julia Tymoshenko, Aamta Tul Waheed, Jack Coggin, Alec Brady, Dominic Bennett, Catherine West, Cameron Brown, Marion Hurst

YOUNG COMPANY
Sara Abanur, Morayo Adekola, Bethany Agaoglu, Afshan Ali, Rizwana Ali, Maryam Al-Jeddal, Matthew Allen, Roni Altman, Bethany Atkins, Willem Babrovskie, Taylor Barnes, Jamie Barton, David Benzoe, Tommy Beswick, Kendal Boardman, Archie Booth, Jacob Brierley, Ellie Burns, James Butterfield, Oceana Cage, Brogen Campbell, Eleanor Cartmill, Gabriel Clark, Thomas Claxton, Joe Clegg, Grace Collard, Grace Collins, Dan Copson, Henry Crabtree, Emily Davies, Alfie Docherty, Terri Donovan, Michael Dwan, Harriet Eaton, Sophie Edwards, Saleh Elgrari, John Featherstone, Aidan Feely, Christian Field, Madison Fijalkowski, Kathy France, Alexandra Gaudel,

James Greenhalgh, Lauren Greer, Martha Hancock, Tom Hardman,Ben Hardy, Joy Hardy, Faye Heywood, Alfie Hibbert, Amber Holt, Adam Hussain, Sam James, Jessica Kaye, Neve Kelly, Martha Kershaw, Hugo Knowles, Elli Kypriadis, Georgia Lea, Elizabeth Logan, Alex Longthorne, Jacob Lucas, Thomas Lyons, Niamh Madden, Matthew Mantel, Sky Marshall, Charlotte Maxwell, Aiden McCarthy, Hannah Mehr, Zoe Ndlovu, Peter Palma, Beth Presswood, Anna Pullar, Kiedis Quigley, Sofia Read, Rose Revitt, Isah-Levi Roach, Emma Robertson, Annie Rogers, James Ryley, Muhammad Saeed, Zakariyya Sajid,Elin Schofield, Noah Shadbolt, Fatma Shami, Catherine Sharples, Aaron Shaw, Charlie Shaw, Katie Shaw, Fabian Smith, Jason Sparrow, Rory Squitieri, Kenya Sterling, Tayiba Sulaiman, Bethany Sykes, Ruby Thirlwell, Anna Ticehurst, Ben Tinniswood, Che Tligui, Fiona Townsley, Ellaika Villegas, Kenan Vurgun, Zahi Wade, Rob Waite, Rose Walker, Michael Ward, Poppy Waxman, Eden Weale, Chloe Weare, Kate Webster, Molly Wilkinson, Lewis Woodward, Emily Woolf, Rebecca Xuan Le, Michael Zoltak

Production Editorial
Michelle Hickman
Programme produced & printed by John Good Ltd

BOARD OF TRUSTEES
Tania Black
(Chair) Ben Caldwell
Tony Gordon
Sinead Greenaway
Cllr Anne-Marie Humphreys
Nicole May
Jean Oglesby
Sally Penni
Jennifer Raffle
Caroline Roberts-Cherry
Bernard Sharp
Geoffrey Shindler OBE
Martyn Torevell
Dave Roscoe
Aziz Rashid
Davina Shah

Honorary Associates (Chairman 1999– 2015) Paul Lee
Honorary Members
Alistair Cox
Peter Folkman
Jack Goldberg
Mike Hutchins
Cllr J King
George Wedell
Keith Whitmore

The Royal Exchange Theatre would very much like to thank Business in the Arts: North West through whose Better Board Bank programme Sinead Greenaway has joined the board.

Patron HRH The Earl of Wessex CVO

DONORS, SUPPORTERS AND BENEFACTORS

PRINCIPAL FUNDERS

MAJOR SPONSORS

manchester
airport

CHEETHAM BELL

PROJECT SUPPORTERS

After Digital
The Andrew Lloyd Webber
 Foundation
Beaverbrooks Charitable
 Trust
The Booth Charities
Arnold & Brenda
 Bradshaw
The Co-operative
 Foundation
Computeam
Duchy of Lancaster
 Benevolent Fund
Esmée Fairbairn
 Foundation
The Eventhall Charitable
 Trust
Galloways Printers
Garfield Weston
 Foundation
The Granada Foundation
Holroyd Howe
Susan Hodgkiss CBE
Jack Livingstone Charitable
 Trust
The John Thaw Foundation
The John Thomas Kennedy
 Charitable Foundation
King Street Townhouse
 Hotel
The Leche Trust
M.A.C Cosmetics
The Madeline Mabey Trust

Manchester Age Friendly
 Neighbourhood
Manchester Guardian
 Society
The Noël Coward
 Foundation
The Oglesby Charitable
 Trust
One Manchester
Ordinary People,
 Interesting Lives
The Paul Hamlyn
 Foundation
The Peter Henriques
 Foundation
Pinsent Masons Foundation
The Raffle Family
The Rayne Foundation
Martyn & Valerie Torevell

PRINCIPAL MEMBERSHIP

Bruntwood
Cheetham Bell
Edmundson Electrical
Regatta

ENCORE MEMBERSHIP

Acies Group
Beaverbrooks
Dewhurst Torevell
DWF LLP
Fieldfisher

ASSOCIATE MEMBERSHIP

Grant Thornton
HFL Building Solutions
Hollins Strategic Land
King Street Townhouse
Hotel
Levitt Bernstein
Mills & Reeve
Pinsent Masons
RSM
Sanderson Weatherall
Sapphire Systems
Smart Alex
Whitebirk Finance Ltd
5plus Architects
UK Together

PATRONS £1000+ PA

Arnold & Brenda
 Bradshaw
Ben & Maggie Caldwell
Meg Cooper
Barbara Crossley
The Harrison Family
Richard & Elaine Johnson
William and Ariel
 Lees-Jones
Sandy Lindsay MBE
Stuart Montgomery
Christine Ovens
Stephen & Judy Poster
& all our anonymous
patrons

Bush
Theatre

Artistic Director	**Madani Younis**
Production Manager	**Michael Ager**
Studio Producer	**Lise Bell**
Theatre Administrator and PA to the Executive	**Arianne Brooks**
Head of Marketing	**Lauren Clancy**
Marketing and Sales Officer	**Lauri Cryan**
Deputy Front of House Manager	**Joseph Denby**
Associate Director	**Omar Elerian**
Digital Marketing Officer	**Rebekah Ellerby**
Bar & Catering Manager	**Isabel da Silva**
Front of House Manager	**Sam Gibbs**
Development Officer	**Poppy Harrison**
Producing Coordinator	**Alison Holder**
Literary Assistant	**Ellie Horne**
Interim General Manager	**Shaun Johnson**
Head of Development	**Sylvain Malburet**
Technician	**Rajiv Pattani**
Associate Dramaturg	**Stewart Pringle**
Technician	**James Swadlo**
Head of Finance	**Candida Ronald**
Development Manager	**Ine Van Riet**
Press Manager	**Martin Shippen**
Community Producer	**Holly Smith**
Interim Producer	**Alex Turner**

Apprentices, Interns and Attachments
Kellie Grogan, Tobi Kyeremateng, Ruthie Osterman, Sita Thomas

Front of House team
Jack Albert-Cook, Isabelle Atkinson, Lucy Atkinson, Arianna Beadie, Jack Byam-Shaw, Rebecca Calf, Beth Church, Ilaria Ciardelli, Guy Clark, Georgina Cornick, Serafina Cusack, Hannah Dunne, James Fletcher, Davey Green, Matias Hailu, Olivia Hanrahan-Barnes, Rukyrah Harris, Rebecca Hyde, Angel Isaacc, Ellie Isherwood, John King, Henry Krempels, Sara Malik, Tim McNiven, Carly Menton, Urielle Klein Mekongo, Simone Mihai, Lily O'Hara, Emily Orme, Ewa Owsiak, Kwame Owusu, Sophie Paterson, Alex Prescot, Philippa Quinn, Molly Skelton, Melissa Stephen, Humaira Wadiwala, Debbie Watson, Katie Webb, Rhea Withero-Taylor

Board of Trustees
Simon Johnson (Chair), Matthew Byam Shaw, Grace Chan, Mark Dakin, Simon Dowson-Collins, Nike Jonah, Khafi Kareem, Isabella Macpherson, Kathryn Marten, Madani Younis

Bush Theatre, 7 Uxbridge Road, London W12 8LJ
Box Office: 020 8743 5050 | Administration: 020 8743 3584
Email: info@bushtheatre.co.uk
bushtheatre.co.uk
The Alternative Theatre Company Ltd
(The Bush Theatre) is a Registered Charity and a company limited by guarantee.
Registered in England no. 1221968 Charity no. 270080

Bush Theatre

We make theatre for London. Now.

The Bush is a world-famous home for new plays and an internationally renowned champion of playwrights. We discover, nurture and produce the best new writers from the widest range of backgrounds from our home in a distinctive corner of west London.

The Bush has won over 100 awards and developed an enviable reputation for touring its acclaimed productions nationally and internationally.

We are excited by exceptional new voices, stories and perspectives – particularly those with contemporary bite which reflect the vibrancy of British culture now.

Located in the newly renovated old library on Uxbridge Road in the heart of Shepherd's Bush, the theatre houses two performance spaces, a rehearsal room and the lively Library Bar.

Supported by
ARTS COUNCIL
ENGLAND

h&f
hammersmith & fulham

bushtheatre.co.uk

THANK YOU

The Bush Theatre would like to thank all its supporters whose valuable contributions have helped us to create a platform for our future and to promote the highest quality new writing, develop the next generation of creative talent and lead innovative community engagement work.

LONE STAR
Gianni Alen-Buckley
Michael Alen-Buckley
Rafael & Anne-Helene Biosse Duplan
Garvin & Steffanie Brown
Alice Findlay
Charles Holloway
Miles Morland

HANDFUL OF STARS
Dawn & Gary Baker
Sofia Barattieri
Martin Bartle
Charlie Bigham
Judy Bollinger
Richard & Lucille Briance
Clive & Helena Butler
Clare & Chris Clark
Clyde Cooper
Zarina Funk
Richard & Jane Gordon
Vera Monotti Graziadei
Madeleine Hodgkin
Priscilla John
Simon & Katherine Johnson
Philippa Seal & Philip Jones QC
V&F Lukey
Georgia Oetker
Philip & Biddy Percival
Clare Rich
Joana & Henrik Schliemann
Lesley Hill & Russ Shaw
Team Nelson
and one anonymous donor.

RISING STARS
ACT IV
Nicholas Alt
Mark Bentley
David Brooks
Catharine Browne
Matthew Byam Shaw
Jennifer Caruso Viall
Tim & Andrea Clark
Sarah Clarke
Claude & Susie Cochin de Billy
Lois Cox
Matthew Cushen
Andrew & Amanda Duncan
Natalie Fellowes & Simon Gresham Jones
Lady Antonia Fraser
Jack Gordon & Kate Lacy
Hugh & Sarah Grootenhuis
Thea Guest
Ann & Ravi Joseph

RISING STARS (continued)
Davina & Malcolm Judelson
Cathy & Paul Kafka
Miggy Littlejohns
Isabella Macpherson
Liz & Luke Mayhew
Michael McCoy
Judith Mellor
Caro Millington
Mark & Anne Paterson
Pippa Prain
Barbara Prideaux
Emily Reeve
Renske & Marion
Sarah Richards
Sophie Silocchi
Susie Saville Sneath
Saleem & Alexandra Siddiqi
Brian Smith
Nick Starr
Peter Tausig
Lady Marina Vaizey
Guy Vincent & Sarah Mitchell
Amanda Waggott
Alison Winter
and three anonymous donors.

SPONSORS & SUPPORTERS
AKA
Alen-Buckley LLP
Gianni & Michael Alen-Buckley
Jeremy Attard Manche
Bill & Judy Bollinger
Edward Bonham Carter
Martin Bowley
Duke & Duchess of Buccleuch
The Hon Mrs Louise Burness
Sir Charles & Lady Isabella Burrell
Philip & Tita Byrne
CHK Charities Limited
Peppe & Quentin Ciardi
Joanna & Hadyn Cunningham
Leo & Grega Daly
Patrick & Mairead Flaherty
Sue Fletcher
The Hon Sir Rocco Forte
The Hon Portia Forte
Mark Franklin
The Gatsby Charitable Foundation
The Right Hon Piers Gibson
Farid & Emilie Gragour
Victoria Gray
John Gordon
Vivienne Guinness
Melanie Hall
The Headley Trust

SPONSORS & SUPPORTERS (continued)
Brian Heyworth
Lesley Hill & Russ Shaw
Madeleine Hodgkin
Michael Holland & Denise O'Donoghue
Graham & Amanda Hutton
James Gorst Architects Ltd.
Simon & Katherine Johnson
Tarek & Diala Khlat
Bernard Lambilliotte
Marion Lloyd
The Lord Forte Foundation
Peter & Bettina Mallinson
Mahoro Charitable Trust
James Christopher Miller
Mitsui Fodosan (U.K.) Ltd
Alfred Munkenbeck III
Nick Hern Books
Georgia Oetker
RAB Capital
Kevin Pakenham
Sir Howard Panter
Joanna Prior
Josie Rourke
Lady Susie Sainsbury
Barry Serjent
Tim & Catherine Score
Search Foundation
Richard Sharp
Susie Simkins
Edward Snape & Marilyn Eardley
Michael & Sarah Spencer
Stanhope PLC
Ross Turner
The Syder Foundation
van Tulleken Family
Johnny & Dione Verulam
Robert & Felicity Waley-Cohen
Westfield London
Elizabeth Wigoder
Phillip Wooller
Danny Wyler
and three anonymous donors.

TRUSTS AND FOUNDATIONS
The Andrew Lloyd Webber Foundation
The Bruce Wake Charitable Trust
The City Bridge Trust
Cockayne—Grants for the Arts
The John S Cohen Foundation
The Daisy Trust
The Equity Charitable Trust
Eranda Rothschild Foundation
Esmée Fairbairn Foundation

TRUSTS AND FOUNDATIONS (continued)
Fidelio Charitable Trust
Foyle Foundation
Garfield Weston Foundation
Garrick Charitable Trust
The Harold Hyam Wingate Foundation
Hammersmith United Charities
Heritage of London Trust
The Idlewild Trust
John Lyon's Charity
The J Paul Getty Jnr Charitable Trust
The John Thaw Foundation
The Leche Trust
The Leverhulme Trust
The London Community Foundation
Margaret Guido's Charitable Trust
The Martin Bowley Charitable Trust
The Monument Trust
Paul Hamlyn Foundation
Pilgrim Trust
The Theatres Trust
Viridor Credits
The Williams Charitable Trust
Western Riverside Environmental Fund
The Wolfson Foundation
and one anonymous donor.

CORPORATE SPONSORS AND MEMBERS
The Agency (London) Ltd
Dorsett Shepherds Bush
Drama Centre London
The Groucho Club
THE HOXTON

PUBLIC FUNDING

If you are interested in finding out how to be involved, please visit **bushtheatre.co.uk/support-us** or email **development@bushtheatre.co.uk** or call **020 8743 3584.**

PARLIAMENT SQUARE

James Fritz

Acknowledgements

Leo Butler, Mel Hillyard, Vinay Patel, Thomas Martin and Emily Wraith, all of whom encouraged me to keep going with this play when it was called something different.

The organisers, readers and judges of the Bruntwood Prize. Brian Quirt, Jenna Rodgers and everyone at the the Banff Playwrights Colony 2016. Madani Younis, Stewart Pringle and everyone at the Bush.

Sarah Frankcom, Matthew Xia and everyone at the Royal Exchange for making me feel so at home in Manchester.

The staff at Whitechapel Ideas Store and John Harvard Library, Borough – the only two places I ever get anything done. Political, public spaces worth fighting for.

And Suzanne Bell and Jude Christian, who made this with me. The two most inspiring, patient dramaturgs a confused writer could ask for. Sorry it took me so long.

J.F.

'Courage calls to courage everywhere,
and its voice cannot be denied.'

Millicent Fawcett

For T.M.
The world got better.

Characters

KAT
TOMMY
TAXI DRIVER
TICKET WOMAN
COLLEAGUE
MUM
DOCTOR
CATHERINE
PHYSIO
FRIEND
FRIEND 2
JO

Note on Text

The two columns of text in Fifteen Seconds are both part of
Kat. How you interpret and stage that is totally up to you.

A line with no full stop at the end indicates an unfinished
thought.

A dash at the end of a line indicates an interruption. A dash at
the beginning indicates someone halfway through a sentence.

*This text went to press before the end of rehearsals and so may
differ slightly from the play as performed.*

ONE

FIFTEEN SECONDS

                                                    Kat.

...

                                                    Get up.

                                                    Kat.

...

                                                  GET UP.

What?

                                              The alarm.

What time?

                                    Turn off the alarm.

Dreaming.

                                      Before he wakes.

Why – ?

Oh.

                                                  Today.

Today is –

                                      Today is THE day.

                                      You slept so well.

Didn't think I

                                Didn't think you would but

Need to get up.

                                      Don't wake him.

Nothing wakes him.

                                        He's a log.

A lump.

Fifteen seconds.

Fifteen seconds.

That's all I have to get through and then –

Get out of bed.

This is the –

Don't think like that get out of bed.

Love these pillows.

They're very soft get out of bed.

This bed.

It's very nice get out of bed.

One more minute.

Now.

Just one more.

I am not fucking about.

One –

**Get up! Get up! Get up! Get up! Get up! Get up!
GEEEEEET UUUUUUP!**

I'm up. I'm up.

Great job.

God.

We're on the way.

On the way.

Can you feel it?

I can feel it. My stomach.

You can feel it and it feels

He's fast asleep.

Good.

Look at him.

That face.

Want to wake him.

Come on.

Say hello.

Don't be thick.

I'm not thick.

The drawer.

You're thick.

Softly.

Top. Jeans.

Those ones.

They'll do.

They're fine.

Except. Maybe?

No.

I mean they're not very –

No.

I know what you're doing.

What?

Delaying.

I'm not.

Delaying the moment you have to –

I just think this top isn't very –

Just take the fucking clothes.

Okay.

Well done.

Now. Out the room.

Okay.

But.

Maybe I should just wake him.

No.

Say something.

Can't just leave him without –

You have to.

He looks so lovely.

Tommy.

My lovely husband.

He's drooling.

He is! He's drooling in his sleep!

On his chin.

Done that since he was a teenager oh bless him.

Look at him.

He's so

disgusting.

Beautiful.

Such a beautifully disgusting man.

I love him so much.

Do you?

Yeah I do yeah I really do.

Okay.

God. I'm gonna miss him. I'm gonna
miss you Tommy.

Oh.

You won't.

I will.

You won't.

Our own little world.

That's what we're like. That's what
Mum always says.

She says a lot of things.

She does yeah.

Come on.

**You think hanging around is gonna
make it easier to go through with this?**

Should say goodbye.

Don't be thick.

Stop saying that.

He'll know something's wrong.

How will he –

He can sense these things on you.

I'm a good liar.

You're a shit liar.

I'm a shit liar.

Stick to the plan.

I want to speak to him.

**Stick to the fucking
plan you idiot.**

**If he gets even a sniff of what
you're planning he'll lock you up
before he lets you leave the house.**

Maybe I need that.

No.

**You got that will-I-won't-I shit out your
system weeks ago and now
you're ready aren't you?**

Wait. He's moving.

Oh shit.

Oh my god he's waking up.

What do I –

TOMMY. *Kat? What time is it?*

I got to go in early today.

Hold it together.

TOMMY. *Why?*

Hold it together.

Team meeting.

He believes you.

TOMMY. *That's shit innit?*

Didn't mean to wake you. Go back to sleep.

Well done.

Can I give him a

Yeah. Okay.

Kiss him.

TOMMY. *Have a nice day.*

I'll see you later.

Say it back.

See you later.

Good.

TOMMY. *Love you.*

Say it.

Love you too.

He's closed his eyes.

Take a moment.

**You're okay. You're strong enough.
You can take this.**

Am I?

You're doing so well.

Oh. Oh.

Fifteen seconds.

That's all you have to get through.

I can do that.

**Course you can because you're
a fucking amazing woman.**

Am I?

You are.

Am I yeah I am.

Thank you.

You're fucking welcome.

Downstairs.

Downstairs. I'm doing this.

You're doing this.

Although –

Wait.

No.

Wait I can't just.

No no.

Jo.

Don't do this to me.

Jo Jo. I can't just go without
saying goodbye to her.

You decided against this.

I know.

Decided it was too hard.

I know I did but

It's torture.

I'll be alright. I promise.

Oh you promise?

I won't wake her up.

So long as you promise.

I'll just. Look at her.

It's a bad idea.

I'm doing it.

It's an awful idea.

I'll be fine. Bedroom. I'll be fine.

Careful.

There she is.

Don't wake her up.

Jo. Hiya Jo.

Quietly.

Ohhh I love her.

She's dreaming.

I'm leaving her.

She'll understand.

She's gonna hate me.

When she's old enough.
She'll get it.

I can't.

Be proud of who her mum is.

I'm a terrible person.

You are the best person.
Look at her.

I can't.

This is the best thing for her.
Hold on to that.
Let's go, eh?

What if I take her with me?

Say goodbye.

I could though couldn't I?
I could take her with me.

Say goodbye.

I could take her with me or
maybe I could I could I could

Say goodbye.

Oh   god.

Please.

Goodbye.

Well done.

Oww.

Owwwwwww.

                              That was hard.

Oh shut up.

                              I know that was hard.

Just shut the fuck up please.

                              But time is ticking.

I need a minute.

                              You haven't got a minute.

IF I SAY I WANT A MINUTE
I CAN TAKE A MINUTE.

                                        Alright.

...

                              That's probably enough now.
                                    Time to get going.

I'm gonna be sick.

                                        No you're not.

Okay. Okay.

                                        You're ready.
                                    Out the front door.

I can't.

                              It's not gonna get any easier.

This house all that time the
things that have happened
the day we moved in the parties
the evenings on the sofa the sex
on the stairs my birthday in the
kitchen pizza and telly in bed

                                            Stop.

The day we came home with her from the hospital.

Leave.

Bye.

Well done.

Forward. That's it.

Garden path. Front gate.

Down the street.

What will the neighbours say
tomorrow? Imagine.

Jesus. I'm doing this

Yeah you are!

I'm doing this.

You're doing this.

I'M DOING THIS!

YOU'RE A SUPERSTAR!

I'M A SUPERSTAR!

Taxi.

There!

Hiya. Station please.

Relax.

My stomach.

TAXI DRIVER. *Want the radio on?*

Answer him.

Okay.

He knows something.

Ridiculous.

He can tell something's wrong
the way he's looking at me.

Calm down.

He knows he knows what
I've got in my bag.

How could he?

TAXI DRIVER. *What time's your train?*

I. I don't know.

Keep calm keep quiet.

I should've walked.

You're fine. Look out the window.

Should've got the bus he knows
he knows I can tell he's gonna stop
me gonna tell someone this is taking
too long I don't know this route it's
too hot in here I need to get out get him
to pull over –

TAXI DRIVER. *Here we are.*

   That's eight pound forty.

Keep the change.

Deep breath.

The station.

The last time we were here.
Holiday. All these people.

Nobody's looking.

Police.

What if they ask to look in my bag?

Why would they?

Don't worry.

I'm not worried.

Alright.

I'm not worried.

Ticket office.

Hi. Could I get a ticket to

TICKET WOMAN. *One way or return?*

One way please.

TICKET WOMAN. *One hundred and
    thirty-five pounds please.*

Is she fucking joking?

That sounds like a lot.

Have a heart attack. Have a stroke.

TICKET WOMAN. *It's the price of a peak ticket.
    If you want to wait until 9 a.m.....*

So smug I hate her.

**Stand your ground! Tell her there's no
    way you're paying that!**

Should I?!

No we've got somewhere to be.

TICKET WOMAN. *Do you want the ticket or not?*

Just pay it.

It's not just my money it's Tommy's money it's –

Grit your teeth.

Yes please.

**That's right. You give her an angry stare.
    That'll show her.**

Think about tomorrow.

> **When she sees the news in a few hours**
> **she's gonna feel so guilty. She'll be eating**
> **her lunch and she'll recognise**
> **you the girl who came to her counter**
> **and she'll realise what you were on your way**
> **to do and she'll feel guilty she didn't give**
> **you the off-peak fare.**
>
> **She'll spend the rest of her life telling**
> **people that she served you on the day**
> **that it happened and she'll be grateful she'll be**
> **so grateful that she served you.**
>
> **She served you on the day that you –**

TICKET WOMAN. *Excuse me.*
  There's a queue behind you.

> **Take your ticket.**

Thank you.

> **Fuck you.**

TICKET WOMAN. *Platform number eight.*

Here we go.

> **Take a breath. That's it.**
> **Take your time.**

Just a normal woman. A normal
woman walking through the
station normally.

Seat to myself.

> **Relax.**

We're moving.

> **You're hungry.**

No.

> **Eat something.**

I wonder if they're awake yet.

Probably not.

Wonder how long it will take him
to realise I'm not at work?

**Might be a while.
He can be a bit slow.**

COLLEAGUE. *Kat?*

Shit.

COLLEAGUE. *Kat!*

Ignore her. Look the other way.

COLLEAGUE. *Thought that was you.*
   What you doing on here?

Oh hiya. Didn't see you.

COLLEAGUE. *I was waving right at you,*
   you were in your own little world.
   Not working today then? Me neither
   I'm not in all week now, lucky for us eh,
   that place'll fall apart without us there you
   watch, although can't get much worse can it?

   Brian never said you were having time off,
   where d'you say you were off to?

I didn't. Visiting family.

COLLEAGUE. *That's nice.*

Be specific.

My aunt's sixty-seventh birthday.

The fuck did that come from?

COLLEAGUE. *Ohhh how nice.*

You don't even have an aunt.

COLLEAGUE. *Tommy not coming?*

No. No he's staying behind.
Looking after Jo. I should –

COLLEAGUE. *Aww. How's she doing little angel?*

She's.

Fine. Yeah.

COLLEAGUE. *Bet you're gonna miss her.*
Always hard leaving them behind at that age.

I. Yeah.

It's alright.

COLLEAGUE. *Remember it well. Didn't*
want to be away from my Peter for
a second when he was two. You feel it
don't you? Instinct kicks in. Course now
he's fifteen I can't wait to get away from him.

Hey. Look at you. You're shaking.

I'm sorry.

COLLEAGUE. *She'll be fine.*
You're not away long are you?

No. Sorry. Not feeling well.

COLLEAGUE. *Here this'll cheer you up.*

Oh no.

COLLEAGUE. *I've told you that*
we're getting a conservatory put in.

Only every bloody day.

COLLEAGUE. *They finished work*
this week that's what it looks like.

Very nice.

COLLEAGUE. *Well it's not much*
but we love it. Somewhere to sit
and read the paper.

What's in the bag?

Sorry?

COLLEAGUE. *In the bag? A present*
for your auntie?

> **Tell her.**

That's right.

> **Tell her what it is.**
>
> **See what she says.**

It's a. A.

> **Well if you're not gonna tell the**
> **truth at least say something.**

A.

> **Been a very long silence now.**

A toolbox.

> **Toolbox? For your**
> **auntie's birthday?**

COLLEAGUE. *Oh. Right. Bit of a DIY*
nut is she?

Yes. She is.

COLLEAGUE. *Toolbox wouldn't*
be much use to my Bill. He wouldn't
know one end of a hammer from the other.

I can't do this.

> **Breathe.**

She's so

> **I know.**

Never shuts up. At work.
Always poking her nose in to
everyone's business always blathering
away about nothing in particular
did you see have you heard so-and-so
said my son Peter

> **And her conservatory.**

And her conservatory you'd think
it was the Sistine fucking Chapel the
way she goes on about it on and on she
goes just blathering chattering away
'*Oooh I know isn't it awful.*' As if that's enough.
Every day every fucking day. We go in and we
work and we talk shit and we all go home and
sit on our sofas and watch it all happen
because it's nothing to do with

It's nothing to do with us.

Maybe I should tell her what I'm gonna do.

You could.

I could, couldn't I?

Imagine her face.

She wouldn't believe you.

She might.

She'd have a heart attack.

Might be impressed.

Might want to do it too.

COLLEAGUE. *Want a biscuit Kat?*

Ooh a biscuit.

COLLEAGUE. *They're a bit melted but
they taste alright.*

No thanks.

I want a biscuit!

COLLEAGUE. *I'm going to go to
the coffee man. Would you like anything?*

You're thirsty.

No thank you.

Ask for some water.

I'm fine.

COLLEAGUE. *Okay, if you're sure.*

Thank you.

> **You know what?**
> **She's actually pretty nice.**

Yeah.

She is.

I feel a bit bad now.

> **You should feel bad.**
>
> **What's that?**

It's Tommy.

> **Oh shit.**

What do I do?

> **You knew he was going to call.**

What do I do?

> **Turn the phone off.**

Decline.

> **He'll keep trying.**

A voicemail.

> **Don't listen.**

TOMMY. *Kat? It's me.*

> **Or just ignore me.**

TOMMY. *Work rang and they said
   you've not come in. So. Just
   wondering where you've got to.
   Give me a call back when you get this.
   Love you bye.*

That's it. That's all he said.

> **Fifteen seconds.**

She's coming back.

> **Close your eyes.**
>
> **Pretend to be asleep.**
>
> **That's –**

COLLEAGUE. *Kat?*

   Kat we're here.

> **What?**

COLLEAGUE. *Didn't want to wake you*
   you looked so peaceful.

> **Oh you actually fell asleep.**

COLLEAGUE. *You slept the whole way!*

Sorry.

COLLEAGUE. *Don't you apologise.*
   I know what it's like when they're young.
   I'll see you back at work next week I spose?

Yeah. Next week.

> **Careful.**

COLLEAGUE. *Enjoy your family do.*

I'm not

> **What you doing?**

I'm not going to a family do.

> **Oh my –**

COLLEAGUE. *I don't understand.*

I lied before.

COLLEAGUE. *Oh. Right.*

> **She looks so sad.**

I'm going to Parliament Square.

> **Come on.**

COLLEAGUE. *Okay.*

I'm gonna stand in the square,
stand in front of that building and

Don't do this.

and take a photo.

COLLEAGUE. *Right*.

Well.

Have a nice time.

What was that about?

Sorry.

Get off the train.

Not been here for years.

I don't remember any of this.

Underground.

So many people.

**You're gonna make things
better for all of them.**

So many.

**So many people and they're all gonna
know your name tomorrow that's –**

*I'm sorry ladies and gentlemen
we're going to be held here due
to a passenger incident on the
tracks up ahead.*

Passenger incident?

Look at their faces.

Person under a train he means.

Late for their meetings.

All those people on that platform
and no one could stop them doing it.
It's so hot in here.

A body under a train. Imagine that.
Imagine seeing that.

Don't think about it.

Imagine being that person.
Would it hurt? Would you feel
it happening?

I said don't think about it.

Or would it just go black would
everything just go black oh god
I'm hot I'm so hot –

Calm down.

I can't breathe.

I'm gonna be sick I've got
to get off.

This isn't our stop?

I've got to get off I've got to
get off now.

Alright go.

Oh god I'm gonna be

Quickly find a

Hooooaah

Lovely.

Oh.

Right on the platform.

You alright mate?

I'm okay. I need air.

Get above ground.
Don't forget your bag!
Fresh air. Breathe. What's that?

Mum.

Don't answer it.

Don't answer it I'm warning you.

Hi Mum.

Dunno why I bother.

MUM. *Hi love. Won't keep you,*
I've just got a quick question
about the weekend.

The weekend.

She doesn't know you're gone.

MUM. *Wondered if you lot*
wouldn't mind coming a bit early,

Hasn't spoken to him.

MUM. *at about two-ish so that*
Tommy can help me get the barbecue going.

The barbecue.

MUM. *Yes love you know I hate doing it*
and he did such a good job last time
and I want it nice and hot by the time
everyone arrives. I know we said later
but two would really help me out.

So two then, on Saturday? I've bought
far too much food.

Two. That's fine.

MUM. *Lovely. Everything else okay*
with you?

Yes. Mum, it's –

MUM. *Okay love got to go.*
See you Saturday. Bye.

Careful.

Bye. Mum.

Sit down.

I –

> **You should sit down.**
>
> **Breathe.**

She –

> **She'll know soon enough.**

> **We should keep going.**

I'm tired.

> **I know.**

I'm really tired now.

> **One foot in front of the other
> that's all you need to do now
> one foot in front of the –**
>
> **No. No. No.**

TOMMY. *Kat. Did you get my last message?*
You're still not at work. Getting a bit worried
now. Give me a ring back.

Kat what the hell do you think you're doing?
You can't just get up and go and not say anything.

> **Stop.**

TOMMY. *Please Kat, call back.*
I'll keep trying.

> **Stop listening to them.**

TOMMY. *Jesus Kat where... where are you.*
I'm starting to really worry now.

Kat, I love you. Please just call me.
I don't care where you are or what
you're doing I just want you to call me.
Please. Jo and me, we're worried about you.

Jo. My little Jo. I wonder if she knows?

How could she?

When she grows up

**Don't think about it
what are you doing?**

When she grows up I wonder
who'll she'll be?

You fucking idiot.

I wonder who her new mum will be?

**Shut up shut up I won't
let you do this.**

What am I doing?

Oh god what am I doing?

Things are good for me. Got a job.
Got a husband who loves me.
A beautiful little girl. Got enough
money to eat, to heat my home.

Got a barbecue at my mum's on Saturday.

So what?

Why me? Why do I have to do it?

**Why not? There's a reason why
you haven't been able to stop –**

There are other people.

Other ways.

**They tried with their anger
their marches their speeches you saw
them thousands on the streets and
then what happened? What?**

I could do something else.

There's nothing else.

I could say something give a speech.

                                          A speech? From you?

Yes.

                                                 Okay.

I could write a good speech.

                    Sure thing. I'm sure everybody will be queueing up to hear that one.

                    Who's gonna listen to what you've got to say? You're no one.

I'm not no one.

I'm a a woman.

                    A woman? What kind of answer is that?

A mum.

                    Everyone's a fucking mum. What else you got?

Fuck you.

                    Fuck you.

                    You might as well have not been born.

No.

That's not true.

                    You're absolutely right.

                    And you know why?

                    Because you're gonna do this.

                    Do something that lasts.

Yes. Okay.

                    You want to change things.

I do I really do.

                    Then come on!

Come on!

                                                    Come on!

COME ON!

                                                    Feel that?

I feel it!

                                                    Feel that inside?

Yeah I do I fucking do.

                          **Focus on that focus on that anger
                          with what's happening that's what
                          will drive you that's what's gonna
                          get you over the line.**

Yes!

                          **Do this and the whole world will listen
                          they will realise that they can't just stand
                          by any more. Your face is
                          gonna go around the world.**

                          **It'll be a beacon of hope on every screen
                          and everyone will be talking about it.**

                                  Your name will ring out.

                                      IT WILL RING OUT.

                                  It will mean something.

                                                    Because.

Because.

I'm going through with it.

                                                    Yes.

                                                    Again.

I'm going through with it.

                                                    Louder.

I'M GOING THROUGH WITH IT
I'M GOING THROUGH WITH IT
I'M GOING THROUGH WITH IT!

It's nice right?

How calm you feel now?

I do. I do feel calm.

Look at the map.

I can walk from here.

One foot in front of the other.

Look.

There.

A post box.

Oh. I almost forgot.

Take out the letter.

Maybe I should check it over?

Make sure it's okay.

You've read it a hundred times.
It's perfect. Post it.

It will work. Won't it?

Of course it will.

It explains everything.

Yes. It does.

Post it. Quick. Before –

It's gone.

Well done.

That's the last thing.

Almost.

It's starting to rain.

Oh my god it's really coming down.

> **Keep going.**

Didn't bring a jacket why didn't I bring
a jacket I'm drenched I'm –

> **It doesn't matter.**

Ugh!

> **Almost there.**

MUM. *Kat, love, it's your mum.*
I just spoke to Tommy. Just give us
a call back to let us know where you are.
We're all a bit worried.

> **Up ahead.**

I can barely see it through the rain.

> **Keep going. Here.**
> **You're here.**

I don't remember it looking like this.
Did it always look like this?

> **Cross the road.**

There's not many people. So many cars.

Oh. Where do I do it?

By the statues?

> **In the middle of the square?**
>
> **I don't know.**

I don't know.

> **You really should've thought**
> **about this before.**

It's Tommy again.

> **Don't answer.**
>
> **Don't do it I'm warning you**
> **don't you dare don't you**
> **dare answer that fucking phone.**

Hi Tommy.

TOMMY. *Jesus Christ, Kat. Thank God*
you're alright. Where are you? I've
been so worried.

Parliament Square.

TOMMY. *What? What the hell are you doing there?*
What's that noise?

It's raining.

TOMMY. *Listen. It doesn't matter.*
Just get back on a train and come
home, eh?

I'm. I'm sorry but. I can't.

TOMMY. *Okay just find somewhere safe*
and I'll come and get you.

No.

TOMMY. *Kat please. I'm coming to get you.*

No don't. I'm not coming home so

TOMMY. *What's going on Kat? You're*
really scaring me now.

I'm sorry.

TOMMY. *We love you. I love you.*

I love you too.

TOMMY. *Then come home eh? Get on*
a train and come back here where it's
warm and dry and we can talk about it,
talk through whatever's bothering you.

I'm so sorry. I have to.

TOMMY. *Kat –*

Come back home to me and Jo.

That's enough now.

I'm. Bye Tommy.

Throw the phone away.

Okay.

Well done.

Owwww.
Owwwwwwwwwwwwwwwwwwwwwwwwwwwww.

I know.

You should get started.

Go into your bag.

Take it out.

The petrol.

Fifteen seconds.

**Fifteen seconds until the fire
burns through the nerve endings
and then you don't feel anything.**

You can count it in your head.

I'm scared.

I'm scared.

I'm really scared.

I'm really scared.

It's gonna hurt.

Fifteen seconds.

It's gonna hurt so much.

**Fifteen seconds and then imagine.
Don't you want to know what it feels like?
What it looks like.**

> **The fire the flames.**
> **Your last experience your most exciting.**

I don't.

> **I don't.**

I don't want to die.

> **I don't want to die.**
>
> **You could just not.**

I could.

> **You could put down the petrol can**
> **and walk away.**

I could.

> **Go home. Kiss him. Watch telly.**

Have a bath. Have sex. Eat a lasagne.

> **Go to your daughter's school.**
> **Go to your daughter's wedding.**

My daughter's –

Jo. Jo.

Yes. I could. I could couldn't I –

> **But you're not going to.**

No. I'm not going to.

> **Say the words.**

I'm going through with this.

> **The hard part's over.**
>
> **I'm excited. I'm so excited!**

The hard part?

> **Fifteen seconds.**
>
> **Look around you.**
>
> **Take it all in.**

Road. Grass. Parliament. Cars. Rain on my face.

Oh my god.

I just. A memory. Came here as
a kid with Mum. We stood right
over there and she took a photo.

                                                        Breathe.

Got an ice cream and took the
boat down the river.

                                                        Breathe.

                                                Take it all in.

Rain. Wind. Concrete. Suits. Cars.
Traffic lights. A fence. A Tesco.
I can see a fucking Tesco!

Of course a fucking Tesco's
one of the last things that I'll see.

                                                    What else?

Statues. Oh god. Police. Flagpoles.
Jo. Her face.

                                                    What else?

Clouds. Oh god.

                                                    What else?

People. Tommy's face. Jo's fingers.
Jo's eyes her smell. People on the street.

                                                     Looking?

They're huddled from the rain they're
looking down they're rushing by.

                                                        Okay.

                                                        Ready?

                                                Think it's time.

One. More. Second.

One more.

                                                  Now or never.

Wind. My face.

                                                  Get it over with.

Okay. Okay.

                                                  Petrol can.

My hands.

                                                  Lid.

Smell.

                                                  Tip it.

It stinks!

                                                  All over.

Stings.

                                                  That's enough.
                                                  Deep breath.

Deep breath.

                                                  You're a hero.
                                                  The lighter.

Where is it?
Can't find my lighter –

                                                  Top pocket.
                                                  Take it out.
                          The last thing you'll ever touch.
                        How does it feel in your hand?

It –

I mean it feels like a fucking lighter.

You're alright.

I'm fine.

Doing great.

You are so brave.

Everyone –

Everyone watching everyone who sees this is going to be changed and they're going to see that when we don't like what's going on we can get up out of our chairs and do something about it. They'll look at the pictures they'll read about what happened and they'll think if that woman can do that I can do something to stop the rot I can do something to stop the rot I can do something I can do something I can do something.

Everyone watching everyone who sees this is going to be changed and they're going to see that when we don't like what's going on we can get up out of our chairs and do something about it. They'll look at the pictures they'll read about what happened and they'll think if that woman can do that I can do something to stop the rot I can do something to stop the rot I can do something I can do something I can do something.

The first fifteen seconds. That's all.

Count to fifteen and it will be just like

Going to sleep.

You. Are. Everything.

Ready?

Yes.

1

2

3

go.

She's on fire.

Fifteen seconds.

My eyes!

One.

Two.

Three

Four.

Hold. On.

Jo.

Five.

Hold on.

Six.

Don't.

Seven.

Scream.

Eight.

She screams.

It is the worst scream we've ever heard.

TWO

FIFTEEN STEPS

Dark.

Silent.

Nothing.

And then.

...

Loud.

Bright.

KAT. *On a bed.*

Her breath rattles and her body shakes violently into life as the whole world shakes violently into life.

What seems like thousands of doctors, nurses, paramedics, anaesthetists buzzing round shouting.

KAT *screams.*

Black.

...

And then. Sunlight.

A hospital room. KAT *on the bed, alone. Her eyes open.*

They close.

Black.

...

Open. TOMMY *and* MUM *look on.* KAT *isolated. Silent.*

TOMMY. Did she. Did she say anything to you?

   Anything that might explain –

A moment.

MUM. No.

TOMMY. What do I –

Close.

...

Eyes open. MUM, TOMMY *and a* DOCTOR.

DOCTOR. – the body shunts all the blood and fluid to the burned area. But when it gets there there's no skin to hold it in, so it leaks out, and without that fluid the kidneys and heart can be in serious danger of giving out.

MUM. Oh Jesus.

DOCTOR. Quick work on arrival meant we were able to get that fluid into her, and get those burns excised early on, which is key to stopping the body going into shock.

So far we've been able to counter any signs of infection. Her temperature's come right down. She's strong your daughter.

MUM. She is.

TOMMY. How. What's she going to look like? When the bandages come off?

DOCTOR. Well. Kat's burns are very severe. The use of the petrol on top of her clothes has resulted in some very deep burns, particularly on parts of the torso and the right arm and leg. After what her body's been through, she's lucky to even be alive. If the fire hadn't been put out so quickly –

MUM. The police said it was just a young girl with her jacket. Did you know that?

DOCTOR. I heard.

MUM. What have they got covering her?

DOCTOR. It's a temporary covering until she's strong enough for the first of the skin grafts.

MUM. It looks so. Strange.

DOCTOR. Well. It's cadaver skin.

TOMMY. A dead body. They've got her covered in a dead man's skin.

Close.

...

Open. TOMMY *alone.*

He doesn't know where to put his hands. Close.

...

Open. KAT *looks around but they don't notice.*

MUM. – on a short-term let. It's no palace, but it'll do. It'll get us out that B and B at least. If I have to talk to that woman one more time.

TOMMY. I still don't see why they can't move her closer to home.

Let me give you some money at least.

MUM. Absolutely not.

Close.

...

Open.

MUM. Oh my god.

Did you see that?

Her eyes her eyes were open.

TOMMY. I didn't see.

MUM. They were Kat love Kat it's me can you –

Close.

...

Open.

DOCTOR. Kat? Kat can you hear me?

TOMMY. Oh my god.

MUM. Oh Kat. Hiya.

TOMMY. Oh my god thank you god thank you.

MUM. I told you, didn't I?

Believe. You've got to keep believing.

...

TOMMY. So.

Jo's fine. She's at my sister's.

You've been out of it for weeks.

There was a moment where we thought –

You should see us. Me and your mum, in this funny little flat together, 'bout half-hour away. I haven't killed her yet, somehow.

Jo. She. She doesn't know what's gone on. Obviously. She knows something's up. But. I'll bring her down when you're feeling a bit better eh?

God I love you. You gave me such a fright.

...

MUM. I fucking hate hospitals.

If I have to have another sandwich from that café.

Call me old-fashioned but I don't think it counts as bacon if it's grey.

Count yourself lucky you're being fed through a drip. There's your silver lining eh?

KAT. M. Mum.

MUM. Hey. Don't worry. Doctor says you're gonna get out of here. We'll get you home.

Once you've had your skin graft and they've started physio.

You scared the shit out of me. Do you know that? Thought we'd lost you. You silly girl.

You were so lucky. If that girl hadn't been there.

KAT. Mum. Did it.

Did it. Work?

MUM. No. No Kat you're still here. Don't worry. You're still alive.

KAT. No.

My letter.

I. I sent you. A letter.

MUM. Get some rest eh?

I'm gonna ask them about getting you a plant or something. Brighten the place up.

...

MUM. You should be very proud you know, Catherine.

CATHERINE. Yeah?

MUM. Young girl like you. Bet your mum's so proud of you.

CATHERINE. Dunno about that.

MUM. Even a moment longer.

CATHERINE. Just glad I was there. I was only a few feet from her I don't think she spotted me. Saw her take out the petrol.

MUM. Okay.

CATHERINE. Splash it on herself. And I was like what is she doing?

MUM. Well.

CATHERINE. You can't just let people die you know. That's what I think anyway. Life's important, innit?

Was funny. Soon as I saw her take the lighter out something in my head just went GO. Like someone else was driving me. You ever get that?

Straight over got my jacket around her didn't even think about it.

Bit of my hair burnt off. Didn't even notice. Adrenalin you know fight or flight. Like you always wonder what you'd be like in those situations don't you and I guess now I know.

MUM. Well you're certainly in our prayers. I mean we're not religious. But you would be. If we were. I don't know why I said that. I'm just gonna hug you.

CATHERINE. Alright!

MUM. I was saying to Tommy. They should give you an award.

CATHERINE. An award.

For me?

No… I mean. Maybe.

MUM. I don't see why not.

You're a hero. How many people would do what you did.

CATHERINE. I did think there was gonna be more about it you know? In the news. Girl saves burning woman or something but –

I looked and couldn't find anything. Not that that's why I did it. But. It would have been nice to have something to show people, you know?

MUM. Your jacket.

It put out the flames.

Must be ruined.

CATHERINE. Oh yeah it's fucked.

MUM. Let me give you some money for it.

CATHERINE. That's okay.

MUM. You're young you need the money. How much was it?

CATHERINE. Don't worry about it.

MUM. Seriously.

CATHERINE. It's fine.

MUM. I want to.

CATHERINE. Two hundred quid.

MUM. For a jacket?

That's. Okay of course that's fine.

CATHERINE. Oh that's so nice. Thank you.

Can I ask you something?

Hope you don't think I'm rude but

Since it happened it's been going round and round my head
and I need to ask.

Why'd she do it?

MUM. What d'you mean?

CATHERINE. Like, why?

MUM. There wasn't a reason.

CATHERINE. Musta been something.

MUM. No.

CATHERINE. So she just did it?

MUM. There's no good reason when someone does something
like this.
She's not well. That's all.

CATHERINE. Oh. Okay.

Why there though? That's all I was wondering. Why that spot?

MUM. Maybe you should come back when she's a bit more
with it, eh?

...

DOCTOR. Hi Kat.

How are you doing today?

I must say we're all very pleased to see you up and awake.

KAT. It hurts.

DOCTOR. Now let me take a look here. And here. Very good. That's good.

This is gonna be a bit.

KAT. Ah!

DOCTOR. A bit sore. There we go. All looks okay to me. You're doing very well. You'll get out of here soon, I promise.

If it helps.

I just wanted to.

What you did.

I mean I'm not really supposed to say anything like this but.

The stuff we see. Put up with. Working here.

The country feels. Sick. And so when I heard about what happened to you.

I understand. I get why. A lot of us here do.

Just thought you should know that. Thought it might help.

Okay.

Now Kat, I'm going to continue checking your dressings, alright? You're going to have to be very brave for me.

DOCTOR *continues checking* KAT's *dressing.* KAT *cries. It is the most painful feeling in the world.*

...

TOMMY. Jo's being as good as gold apparently.

KAT. Jo.

TOMMY. I'll bring her in soon. I promise.

We thought we'd wait until you were feeling up to it before we brought her.

They said I should take some pictures of you. To show her. To help her adjust so it's not so much of a shock when she –

Maybe later eh?

KAT. Tommy –

TOMMY. So you know. I've told people back home you had an accident. Cooking.

KAT. What. Why?

TOMMY. I've been thinking and.

I don't want you to tell me why you did this.

I don't want us to talk about that.

Ever. Okay?

I won't ask you. And I don't want you to tell me. Because I can't –

Okay.

Let's just get you better.

...

KAT. Mum. I haven't seen anything. In the news.

MUM. Well. You seem perkier.

KAT. What's going on has anything happened?

MUM. You've been in here for weeks. Lots has happened.

There's nothing to worry about if that's what you mean.

KAT. People saw me people must have seen me.

MUM. You were lucky the whole thing didn't last for very long.

KAT. No. No no.

Mum I posted you a letter explaining. Asking you to tell people. Tell Tommy. But he doesn't

MUM. There was no letter love. I'm sorry. Are you sure you aren't confused?

KAT. No!

MUM. The doctors say that you might be a bit confused about events that day.

KAT. No no no this doesn't make sense.

I need to get out of here.

MUM. Settle down.

KAT. I need to get out help me get out. I need to tell people.

I need to

I need to

KAT *breaks*.

MUM *holds her daughter*.

It was all for nothing it was all for nothing it was all for nothing it was all for nothing.

MUM. It's alright. Love. It's alright. I'm here. I'm here. I've got you. I'm here.

...

PHYSIO. Hiya Kat.

How you feeling today?

Nothing? That's okay I get that a lot.

So I thought I'd come say hi as I'm going to be doing physio with you twice a day over the next few weeks. I know right. Lucky you.

See this face? Nice innit. Get a good look because in a few days you're gonna hate it. It's alright, I won't take it personally. You're gonna hate this face because it's going to make you do a lot of things that you don't want to do. A lot of things that are going to be quite painful. But it's only through doing those things that we're gonna get you up and about alright? Get you walking.

I'm going to need you to believe in me and trust that I know what I'm doing. Can you do that Kat? Work through the pain, work together, and we'll get you to the end of this.

...

TOMMY. I'm going back home. I need to be back at work and.

My sister's had Jo too long and.

And I can't be here any more Kat. I'm sorry but I just. Can't.

I think if I stay I won't be able to stop myself asking why.

And that's. That's not.

Because I've tried not to get angry.

Get upset.

But. You got up. And you left me. Without saying a word. Without even saying goodbye.

One moment I thought things were fine and the next you're on the phone and.

And that's why I'm gonna go. For a bit. So I can. Think. You know? Calm down. Because I want to help you get through this. I do.

Life is a very

I mean it's a gift isn't it? That's what they say and

This world. Well. It's not so bad is it? There's actually a lot of good in it. If you look. There's value in all of our lives. That's what I think anyway.

And I think. Hope. That we can be. That I can still make you. Happy.

And so it doesn't matter why you did this. What matters is

Anyway. I love you.

I'll be back soon.

...

PHYSIO. How are we doing today? Feeling good? Ready to get started on some physio!?

No?

Nothing? Just gonna leave me stood here talking to myself? That's fine.

I find myself pretty charming company actually.

Hello mate how are you today I'm fine thanks for asking.

I can wait all day.

Well not all day I have other appointments.

But a while. I can wait a while.

Okay. We'll try again tomorrow.

···

DOCTOR. Where's your lovely husband then? Haven't seen him in a few days.

KAT. Please. You said you understood why I did. What I did.

DOCTOR. I'm sorry?

KAT. You told me you understood.

Nobody knows that it happened. Can you help me? Maybe you can contact a journalist or –

DOCTOR. Oh. Um. I don't think that would be.

KAT. Or you could take a photo and share it maybe?

DOCTOR. That's not really allowed I'm afraid.

KAT. But you said –

DOCTOR. I think you're mixing me up with someone else.

Listen. I'm really sorry. I would if I could.

Keep up your physio. Keep working.

You'll be out of here in no time.

···

PHYSIO. Right Kat. What's say we try again eh?

KAT. I'm sleeping.

PHYSIO. You can sleep. You can stay in that bed forever if you like. Well maybe not that bed. We need that bed. But a bed. Somewhere.

Or I can get you up and you can get on with the rest of your life.

Get you walking again. It's up to you.

You want to get out of here don't you?

There must be something you want to do out there? Right?

Something you want to achieve?

There is.

KAT. Yes.

PHYSIO. What is it?

That's fine you don't have to tell me.

Just so long as you're ready to get started.

Okay.

···

KAT. I can't I can't do it I don't want to do it.

PHYSIO. I know you don't but I'm gonna make you so...

KAT. Ohhhh I fucking hate you.

PHYSIO. I hate you back. Three steps.

KAT. Fuck you.

PHYSIO. Fuck you.

Three steps. One. That's it. Two.

From there to me. Come on. Come on!

Three. Well done. Well done you.

···

KAT. Seven?

PHYSIO. Seven.

KAT. I thought it was three.

PHYSIO. It was three yesterday.

KAT. No.

PHYSIO. It's seven today.

KAT. No way.

PHYSIO. Seven today fifteen by the end of the week.

KAT. I'm not doing seven you can shove seven up your arse.

PHYSIO. That was the deal. Three yesterday. Seven today.

KAT. And fifteen. It'll take me months to get to fifteen.

PHYSIO. End of the week. Come on.

KAT. It's too many.

PHYSIO. One.

KAT. God.

PHYSIO. Two.
Three. That's it.

KAT. It hurts.
Just let me. Rest here for a second.

PHYSIO. You're doing so well.

Come on. Four!

KAT. Why do you do this?

PHYSIO. It's my job.

KAT. That's not an answer.
I won't keep going until you tell me.

PHYSIO. Come on.

KAT. Fine. I'm done. Four steps is enough.

PHYSIO. Alright. You really want to know?
I'm going to ask you a question.

KAT. Ask away.

PHYSIO. It's going to sound quite blunt.

KAT. Okay.

PHYSIO. And I don't expect you to say yes.

KAT. That's fine.

PHYSIO. Have you accepted the Lord Jesus Christ as your
personal saviour?

KAT. Oh my god you're one of them.

PHYSIO. It's just a question.

KAT. Nurse! Nurse!

PHYSIO. You don't have to say yes.
I'm not here to convert you.

KAT. No I haven't accepted Jesus as my personal saviour.

PHYSIO. Well I have. And that's why I'm here.

KAT. Jesus told you to become a physiotherapist?

PHYSIO. Let's not give him too much credit. He told me
I should be helping people. I filled in the blanks.

KAT. And he still talks to you?

PHYSIO. Every day.

KAT. Well. That must be nice for you.

PHYSIO. You don't have to believe to understand what I'm
talking about.

He gives me a drive to become a better person. The bad news
for you is that drive also makes me a stubborn prick.
A stubborn prick who's not going to leave you alone until
you do seven steps.

Five.

Six.

...

CATHERINE. I came before but you were asleep.

Met your mum. She's fun. Wanted to come. Say hello. Check
you were alright.

It's good to see you out of bed though. You look better.

KAT. Who are you?

CATHERINE. You don't remember me?

Oh shit.

Sorry.

I came before but you were a bit. My name's Catherine. Nice to meet you.

I'm the one who saved you. Saved your life you know?

KAT. You.

CATHERINE. Me.

I'm the one who put you out. Didn't they tell you I was coming?

KAT. No.

CATHERINE. They said they were gonna tell you.

KAT. No.

CATHERINE. I ran over and put you out with my coat don't you remember? You were properly on fire and I ran over.

Look. You don't need to thank me. I'm just glad to see you're alright. Some people been saying I'm a hero or whatever but I just call that being a human being you know.

So how you doing? You doing okay? Your mum says you're doing loads better.

You got a nice room. Do you like it?

KAT. You stopped me?

CATHERINE. That's right.

KAT. Why?

CATHERINE. I'm sorry?

KAT. Why did you stop me?

CATHERINE. I don't understand.

KAT. You stopped me before anyone could see.

CATHERINE. Before –

Of course I did. You'd have died.

KAT. You had no right.

CATHERINE. I saved your life.

KAT. No fucking right.

CATHERINE. I'm sorry.

Are you angry?

KAT. Get out.

CATHERINE. Maybe I should go.

KAT. Get the fuck out of here!

CATHERINE. I'm. I'm going.

It was nice to meet you properly.

...

MUM *and* KAT.

KAT. Mum. I want you to do something for me.

MUM. Alright.

KAT. I want you to film me.

MUM. Film you? Doing what?

KAT. Show my bandages, my scars, and. I'll explain what happened to the camera. Explain why I did it.

MUM. Oh Kat love.

I know why you did it.

I've read the letter you posted.

KAT. What.

MUM. It was waiting for me when I got home. That first terrible weekend when we weren't sure if you were ever going to wake up. I went home to pick up some things and it was sitting for me on my doormat.

Can I ask you something?

Why did you send it to me of all people?

KAT. I thought you'd understand.

MUM. Understand? I'm disgusted.

  I burnt that letter soon as I read it. Police were already
  asking questions. Tommy was distraught. Didn't want
  anyone else knowing about it if they didn't have to.

KAT. You should have told someone.

MUM. Then what? It makes the news and suddenly it all stops
  praise be our problems are solved because one woman's tried
  to top herself?

KAT. No. I don't know.

MUM. Look what you've done to yourself. And now you sit
  here and you say you want me to film you looking like –

KAT. I'm asking you –

MUM. I'm your mother. Imagine if it was you sat here and Jo in
  the bed burnt half to death.

  And Tommy.

  I've sat here. The whole time. Not been able to tell him he's
  been put through hell so you could do some sort of stunt or –

KAT. No. Not a stunt.

  I couldn't just sit around watching the news any more.

  I had to do something Mum.

MUM. What's wrong with a fucking petition!

  What about Jo? Did you even think about her?

KAT. Of course.

MUM. What she'd feel?

KAT. I did it for her.

MUM. Don't say that. Don't you say that.

KAT. It's her world too and people are suffering.

MUM. So what Kat? So what? They're strangers. She's your
  daughter.

I know I've not always been the best mother. But I would
never have abandoned you. Never. Not for anything.

I would rather have seen a million strangers die screaming
and hungry than have ever left you on your own. Have ever
seen you get

Hurt.

And that doesn't make me a bad person. It makes me human.
Look at your face. You're in agony.

And it didn't change a damn thing.

You want to change the world? You can do a hell of a lot more
alive than dead my girl, don't you see? You could dedicate the
next forty years of your life to changing things, if you wanted
to. Now that's a lot harder. It'll take a lot more graft and it's a
lot less showy. But it's a damn site more effective.

KAT. I had to Mum. I had to do this.

MUM. You didn't darling. And that's what breaks my heart.

KAT. I'll tell Tommy.

MUM. No.

KAT. He might understand.

MUM. No!

I want you to listen to me. Really listen to me.
The world is a terrible place. But guess what? It always
has been.
I've fought against things like this since before you were born.

But you know the thing about all those times? I wasn't by
myself. We fought together. And we lost. Over and over
again we lost. Oh boy. But we did it together.

No one ever changed the world alone. Not in this country.
We're not wired that way. You've got to believe in other
people.

When someone does something like this we don't see a hero.
We see a lunatic. I'm sorry to say it but that's just the way it is.

KAT. If I don't tell anyone, it's all for nothing.

MUM. Oh Kat. It's already for nothing.

Tommy's coming back down next week. You know that boy is never going to understand why you did this. And he shouldn't have to.

Whatever drove you to do this, I want you to forget all about it. You bury it down deep and you move on. You don't tell anyone.

Kat. Are you listening to me?

Whenever anyone asks you what happened you look them in the eye and you lie. You lie with all your heart.

And you get out of here. Get better. Go back to living your life. To raising that little girl.

KAT. Mum –

MUM. Family. Happiness. That's all that matters, really. We get a little bit of happiness and then we die.

I love you so much.

My beautiful little girl.

KAT. You had no right.

MUM. I know I didn't.

But I'm your mum. So.

...

KAT *and the* PHYSIO.

PHYSIO. You ready? This is it. Fifteen steps from you to me.

KAT. Okay.

One step.

PHYSIO. Good. Two.

Two steps.

Three steps.

You're doing so well.

Four steps.

KAT. Ah fuck. Fucking fuck.

Five steps.

PHYSIO. Four. Five. Kat look at me. Focus on each movement.

Six steps.

That's it. You've got it in you Kat I know you do.

Seven steps.

Focus. Focus on all the things you're going to do when you get out of here. Let that drive you let that get you over the line.

Eight steps.

All the things you're going to do on the other side of those doors.

Nine steps. TOMMY *enters.*

TOMMY. Hiya Kat.

KAT. Tommy.

KAT *falters.*

TOMMY. Sorry. Keep going. Don't mind me.

PHYSIO. It's alright. We can stop.

KAT. No.

TOMMY. I'll stay out of the way.

PHYSIO. Do this you can do anything come on Kat. Six more.

Ten steps.

Come on. Take your time. Five left.

TOMMY. Keep going.

PHYSIO. Keep going Kat. Think of all the things you're going to be doing. Think of getting out of here and going home. Doing whatever you want.

Eleven steps.

Twelve.

Thirteen.

KAT *falters.*

KAT. I can't. No more.

It's too hard.

She breaks down.

TOMMY *rushes to catch her.*

TOMMY. Hey. Hey. It's alright. I've got you.

Two more.

He helps her take a step.

That's it.

Last one.

KAT. Tommy.

I'm sorry.

I'm so sorry.

Take me home.

...

THREE

FIFTEEN YEARS

TOMMY *and* KAT *arrive home.*
It's still difficult for KAT *to walk.*
TOMMY. Welcome home Kat.
KAT. Tommy.

    Let's shut out all the rest of it.

– The world gets worse. –

TOMMY *applies lotion to* KAT*'s burns.*
TOMMY. Every day that's what he said.

– The world gets worse. –

KAT. It hurts. Tommy.
TOMMY. I'm here.
KAT. Jo.
TOMMY. She's fine.

– The world gets worse. –

TOMMY. We don't have to see them if you don't –

– The world gets worse. –

KAT. I was cooking on the hob and the robe just went up.

FRIEND. Awful. Just awful.

KAT. Tommy saved me. Put me out. Didn't you?

TOMMY. Yeah.

– The world gets worse. –

KAT. Tommy. Wake up. I'm hot. I'm so –

TOMMY. Wait there –

KAT. Water I need –

– The world gets worse. –

TOMMY *applies lotion to* KAT*'s burns.*

KAT. Thank you. That feels –

– The world gets worse. –

TOMMY *and* KAT. Happy birthday dear Jo-o!

– The world gets worse. –

KAT. She doesn't want to be around me.

TOMMY. Hey. Of course she does.

KAT. The way she looks at me it's.

– The world gets worse. –

TOMMY. More money.

KAT. You always said –

TOMMY. I know. But it's more money. I might enjoy it.

– The world gets worse. –

TOMMY. You're shivering.

KAT. I'm fine.

TOMMY. I'm calling the doctor

KAT. I'm fine –

– The world gets worse. –

KAT. I was cooking. On the hob.

FRIEND 2. And Tommy –

TOMMY. I was in the other room and I ran in and put out the fire.

KAT. That's right.

– The world gets worse. –

KAT. I can't fight with you any more Mum.

MUM. Okay. Well I'm glad.

KAT. I just want to forget about all of it. Like you said. Is that okay?

MUM. Okay.

Just be happy love. That's all I want for you.

It's good to have you home.

– The world gets worse. –

KAT. How was it?
TOMMY. Good. Yeah. Far as first days go.
   Bit boring but –

– The world gets worse. –

KAT. How was work?
TOMMY. How you feeling?

– The world gets worse. –

KAT. – you doing I told you not to come home.
TOMMY. I'm taking you to the hospital. No argu–

– The world gets worse. –

MUM. – being paranoid.
TOMMY. All due respect but she's not your daughter.
MUM. Tell him he's being paranoid –
KAT. I agree with –

– The world gets worse. –

FRIEND. – looking great. Isn't she?
TOMMY. She is.

FRIEND. You thought about what I said?

Thank god you were there Tommy but the robe you were wearing should've been flame retardant.

Get a lawyer. Go to the press.

TOMMY. You might be right.

FRIEND. What if it happens to someone else? A little kiddy whoosh.

Flame retardant I'm –

– The world gets worse. –

COLLEAGUE. Kat. It's so good to see you.

When I heard about what happened –

TOMMY. Her robe. On the hob.

COLLEAGUE. I heard. Awful. The last time I saw you it was on the train.

KAT. It happened a few days later.

COLLEAGUE. Right.

KAT. Tommy put me out.

TOMMY. I put her out.

COLLEAGUE. Is that right?
Well. You're a bit of a hero aren't you. Thank god you were there.

It's good to see you up and about.
Are you thinking of coming back into work? We all miss you.

TOMMY. No.

KAT. Maybe.

COLLEAGUE. Right.

TOMMY. We're going to talk about it.

– The world gets worse. –

EVERYONE. Happy birthday dear Jo-o!

– The world gets worse. –

TOMMY. How was work?

KAT. Great. Really great.

TOMMY. You're not too –

– The world gets worse. –

MUM. – don't see what the big deal is.

KAT. I don't want the news on around her.

MUM. She doesn't understand.

KAT. The images. The things they –

– The world gets worse. –

COLLEAGUE. Isn't it awful? Those poor kids. I'm putting the
    kettle on you want something?

Makes you realise how lucky we are when you see footage
    like that. My son Peter –

– The world gets worse. –

KAT. I like working.

TOMMY. I just don't see why we should jeopardise your health when we don't need the money.

I'm doing great, everyone says so. Few more years like this and –

– The world gets worse. –

EVERYONE. Happy birthday dear Jo-o! Happy birthday to –

– The world gets worse. –

TOMMY. – in the other room watching telly and I heard this awful scream. I'll never forget that sound for as long as I live. Shouting my name weren't you? Of course instantly I knew what had happened don't know how sometimes you just know don't you? And I ran faster than I've ever run before and I just acted. You know? I grabbed this picnic blanket we had lying around from the weekend thank god it was there and I wrapped it round her until the flames were out and I just held her. Doctors said even a moment longer –

– The world gets worse. –

KAT. I'll get some ice.

TOMMY. Group of lads jumped him.

KAT. God.

TOMMY. Second time this month.

– The world gets worse. –

COLLEAGUE. Isn't it awful?

KAT. Yeah.

COLLEAGUE. I've given some money.

KAT. That's good.

COLLEAGUE. Well you've got to do something don't you?

KAT. Yeah. You do.

– The world gets worse. –

TOMMY *rubs lotion into* KAT*'s burns.*

– The world gets worse. –

TOMMY. – a takeaway? Or we could –

– The world gets worse. –

KAT. Hurts a bit when –

– The world gets worse. –

EVERYONE. Happy birthday dear Jo-o! Happy birthday to –

– The world gets worse. –

CATHERINE. You got somewhere we could talk?

KAT. How did you find me?

CATHERINE. Your name's on the company website. I've been waiting for hours.

You look well.

Can we go inside.

KAT. No.

CATHERINE. The last time I saw you –

KAT. I wasn't well.

CATHERINE. No that's okay.

I needed to come to see you. To say sorry. I should never have put you out. It wasn't my place.

KAT. There's no need.

CATHERINE. Please.

I can't stop. Picturing it. You on the grass. On fire. Orange on green.

When I got home from the hospital that night I was so shook up. You were so angry and I couldn't work out why. Because it's a good thing what I did it's supposed to be a good thing. Saving someone's life.

And I started to think. What it was for? Why was she doing it? I tried to imagine what it could have been. Looking for reasons. And the more I looked the more reasons I found.

I can't stop watching the news. Reading everything I can.

I need to know.

What was it made you do it?

Like, what was the reason?

Was there a reason?

What made you do it?

Why did you do it Kat? Please. I just want to know. I could tell people maybe tell your story talk about what happened –

KAT. No. Nobody knows what happened that day. We've told everyone it was an accident. Please don't tell anyone.

Forget about it. We have.

I have to go.

CATHERINE. I'm sorry. I'm so sorry.

KAT. Don't ever contact me again.

– The world gets worse. –

EVERYONE. Happy birthday dear Jo-o!

– The world gets worse. –

FRIEND. This area's really gone downhill. We've started
looking for a new place.

– The world gets worse. –

KAT. Jo! Dinner's ready!

– The world gets worse. –

EVERYONE. Happy birthday dear Jo-o! Happy birthday to you!

– The world gets worse. –

KAT. Jo! I think Santa's been...

– The world gets worse. –

EVERYONE. Happy birthday dear Jo-o!

– The world gets worse. –

KAT. Jo you get down here *right* now.
KAT *and* TOMMY. JO!

– The world gets worse. –

EVERYONE. Happy birthday dear –

– The world gets worse. –

KAT. Jo! Jo! Jo!

JO. Oh my god Mum? You okay?

KAT. I'm fine love. Just a bit. Give me a hand.

JO. Sit down.

   Shall I get you some water?

KAT. Thank you. Yes.

JO. I'm calling the doctor.

KAT. No. I'll be alright in a minute. Go and get on with your
   homework.

JO. Here.

KAT. Thank you. You're a good girl.

– The world gets worse. –

KAT. What did they say?

JO. Doesn't matter.

KAT. Were they making fun?

JO. They won't do it again.

– The world gets worse. –

MUM. Were you even listening to me?

KAT. Sorry Mum?

TOMMY. Sorry what?

MUM. You two. You're in your own –

– The world gets worse. –

FRIEND. I know they're all angry but the more they behave like that the less people are going to listen to what they have to say.

TOMMY. You're right. I was saying that exact same thing to –

– The world gets worse. –

EVERYONE. Happy birthday dear Jo-o!

– The world gets worse. –

MUM. – won't stop long I just wanted to see if you two were free for the barbecue on Sunday.

KAT. You want Tommy to –

– The world gets worse. –

JO. This is really good Mum.

– The world gets worse. –

MUM. – snatched it right out of my hand the animal. Luckily
there was a policeman nearby and they were able to catch the
guy. Bag was long gone though.

TOMMY. This area. Haven't I been telling you?

– The world gets worse. –

TOMMY. I got it!

KAT. Oh Tommy that's wonderful! Congratulations!

TOMMY. This is gonna make such a difference to us, you watch.

– The world gets worse. –

JO. I hate you! It's not fair!

KAT. Well, the world's not fair.

– The world gets worse. –

TOMMY. They were out there again last night. We've got to
move.

JO. I'm not moving.

TOMMY. We can afford better now.

KAT. You really think

JO. I'm not fucking moving.

KAT *and* TOMMY. Hey!

– The world gets worse. –

MUM. – it's very nice. Those exposed beams.

TOMMY. Gate out front. Guard's there twenty-four hours.

KAT. Closer to my new doctor.

TOMMY. See that alarm system? State of the art. Can be here in fifteen minutes –

– The world gets worse. –

COLLEAGUE. Cut him down right in the street. Couldn't believe it.

How's your new place?

– The world gets worse. –

EVERYONE. Happy birthday to you. Happy birthday to you. Happy birthday dear Jo-o!

– The world gets worse. –

EVERYONE. Dear Jo-o!

– The world gets worse. –

EVERYONE. Dear Jo-o!

– The world gets worse. –

EVERYONE. Dear Jo-o!

– The world gets worse. –

KAT. Jo!

JO. I'm coming. Jesus.

– The world gets worse. –

KAT. You come straight home once it's finished. And don't talk
    to anyone. Let me give you some money for a taxi.

JO. Mum. I'll be fine.

KAT. Do not get the bus under any –

– The world gets worse. –

MUM. Hundreds of them. Suffocated.

KAT. Mum –

JO. I don't mind.

MUM. She needs to know.

KAT. I don't want her hearing those stories.

JO. I'm fine.

MUM. She's gonna find out about it one way or another.

TOMMY. We think it's best if –

– The world gets worse. –

EVERYONE. Happy birthday dear Jo-oooo!

– The world gets worse. –

TOMMY. Kettle's on.

– The world gets worse. –

KAT. – say that nobody above the thirteenth floor made it out.
TOMMY. I'm amazed it hasn't happened before.

– The world gets worse. –

TOMMY. – there's no excuse for that sort of behaviour. They
   look like a bunch of bloody animals. A lot of those windows
   belonged to local businesses. It's not the local businesses'
   fault. I'm sorry but –

– The world gets worse. –

EVERYONE. Happy birthday dear Jo-o! Happy birthday to you!
MUM. Give your nana a kiss then.
JO. Aw Nan. Get off.

– The world gets worse. –

KAT. Thank you for seeing me.
CATHERINE. Okay.

KAT. I wanted to talk to you.

> I was horrible to you and I've regretted that ever since.
> I owe you everything Catherine. I never thanked you for that.

CATHERINE. No.

KAT. So thank you. Deeply.
> You don't look. Are you alright?

CATHERINE. Things are difficult.
> Everything is very difficult.

KAT. Do you need money?

CATHERINE. No. That's not.
> What are you doing here?

KAT. My daughter still doesn't know. She thinks I had an accident.

CATHERINE. You should tell her. She should know who her mum is.

KAT. I can't have her knowing. You understand?

CATHERINE. I should've let you burn.

KAT. Don't say that.

> I've seen my daughter grow up. Shared happiness with my husband. I'm living a good life and it's all thanks to you and I'm sorry I haven't said that before.

> Stopping me was the right thing to do.

CATHERINE. For you maybe. But for the rest of us?

> I live that day over and over. What you looked like. Smelt like. What made you do it.

> You saw all this coming and tried to do something about it. And I stopped you. And every day when I see whatever shitty thing has happened that morning I'm reminded of it.

> If I hadn't been there you might have changed everything. Stopped the rot before it set in.

KAT. I wasn't well.

CATHERINE. You don't actually believe that do you?

You weren't mad. You were just ahead of the curve. You thought things were bad then. Look at them now. It's a wonder people aren't burning themselves every day.

Fifteen years on and everything's just got worse and worse and we still haven't hit the bottom. We just keep on burrowing into the shit.

But it's alright.

Because I'm –

– The world gets worse. –

KAT. This is our house.
You can't just go letting homeless men in our kitchen.

JO. He was hungry. It's called being a human.

KAT. We could have been robbed. You could have been killed.

JO. Don't be so dramatic.

KAT. If you ever do something like that again.

JO. Just because you don't give a shit about the rest of the world doesn't mean the rest of us can't –

KAT *slaps* JO.

KAT. I'm sorry.

I'm so sorry. I shouldn't have done that.

JO. I thought I was doing a good thing.

KAT. I know.

You were.

Of course you were.

– The world gets worse. –

KAT. Thank you for coming, we really appreciate you all giving up your evenings.

I'll try and keep this short, because I know you all want pudding. God, I don't know where to start. Tommy always makes these things look easy.

There was a time when I never thought I'd see a day like today. If you told me I'd be standing here giving a toast to my husband I'd never have believed you in a million years. Any of you who knew Tommy at fifteen will understand.

When we first got together my mum would hate it. She'd be talking at us, asking us to do something. Take the bins out or do the washing up. And we just wouldn't hear her would we Mum? 'You're in your own little world you two.' That's what she always used to say. And she was right.

Because when I was with Tommy, nothing else mattered. And then we had Jo. And she mattered even more to us than we did to each other. If that was possible.

It hasn't always been easy. I haven't always been easy. But he has always taken care of me and he's given me a wonderful life and –

Happy anniversary.

Enjoy yourselves. And please, keep eating. There's far too much food.

To Tommy.

And to our little world.

– The world gets worse. –

MUM. The doctors have all been wonderful. Don't have to tell you about that.

I keep thinking, I wish I believed in an afterlife.

That'd be nice. That any day now it's going to be all blue sky and frozen margaritas. Instead of just...

KAT. Oh Mum.

MUM. Don't worry about me.

Maybe it's the right time to go eh? Everything's falling apart out there. My body sympathises.

Here.
I've got something for you.

MUM *takes out the letter* KAT *sent her.*

I know I said I destroyed it but. Well. There you go.

Passes it over.

KAT. You kept it? Why?

MUM. I'm sorry I ignored it. I'm sorry that I told you to lie about why you did. What you did. For so long.

I should never have done that.

KAT. No, Mum. You were right to. What good would it have done, anyone knowing?

MUM. I was so angry when I read that. I hated you for doing that to yourself. To your family. To me.

But despite that. Despite the anger and fear and sorrow that came into our lives that awful day. There was still a part of me that couldn't help feeling it was. Brave.

I mean it was fucking stupid. And selfish. So selfish. And I've wished every day from that one to this that you hadn't done it.

But. Brave.

I thought you should know that I always thought that.

KAT. Mum. Why did you keep this?

MUM. That's my daughter in those pages.

It's late.

I'm tired. Aren't you tired?

– The world gets worse. –

TOMMY. Hey. How you doing?

KAT. Okay.

TOMMY. What have you got there?

KAT. It's.

It's nothing. A letter I wrote to Mum, a long time ago.

I found it clearing out her bedroom.

TOMMY. I want you to know. Whatever you're feeling, whatever's going on in that head. You're not alone.

KAT. I know that.

TOMMY. And if you need to talk about your mum. Or. Anything.

I just want to make sure you're not thinking of. Or feeling –

KAT. Tommy. I'm okay.

TOMMY. Okay. Good.

What does the letter say?

KAT. I can't bring myself to read it yet.

Hey.

Come here.

Thank you. Thank you so much for everything.

– The world gets worse. –

KAT *alone. With the letter.*

She stares at it.

She screws it up without opening it.

A moment.

She changes her mind. Unfolds the screwed-up ball. Opens the letter.

She sits down and reads every word.

Finishes.

Something happens.

– The world gets worse. –

KAT *and* JO.

JO. Why didn't you tell me before?

KAT. I am so sorry.

JO. You should have told me.

KAT. I know.

   Are you okay?

JO. Dad knows?

KAT. He knows it wasn't an accident. Where it happened.
   He doesn't know why I.

JO. Why?

KAT. He never wanted me to tell him.

JO. No. Why did you do it?

   You wanted to kill yourself?

KAT. I don't know.

JO. Mum.

KAT. Yes. I did.

JO. Why?

   You were depressed?

KAT. No.

JO. Sick?

KAT. No. It's hard to explain.

JO. Try.

KAT. The world was getting worse and I wanted.

Needed. To.

Do something.
I wanted you to have a world that wasn't –

JO. I'm fine. The world is fine.

KAT. I know. I know you are.

Here.

She takes out the letter. Passes it to JO.

I wrote that to your nan on the day that I did it. Explaining.

Your dad's never seen it. Doesn't know it exists. I want you to read it.

You should know who your mum was. Is.

But when you read it I want you to remember.

Someone put out the fire. They saved my life. And not a day goes by when I'm not thankful that they did.

– The world gets worse. –

Parliament Square.

KAT *arrives.*

The bells chime.

It starts to rain. She sees CATHERINE. *She is holding a can of petrol.*

KAT. Catherine.

Why don't you put down the petrol?

CATHERINE. What are you doing here?

Didn't tell you to come. That's not why I told you.

KAT. I know that.

CATHERINE. You really shouldn't be here. I've made up my mind.

This is the spot right? Where you did it?

KAT. Close enough.

CATHERINE. You been back here since?

KAT. No.

CATHERINE. Must be strange.

CATHERINE *opens the petrol can.*

KAT. Wait –

Please.

CATHERINE *pours petrol all over herself. It stinks.*

CATHERINE. Stay back.

KAT. If you're doing this for me –

CATHERINE. I'm not.

KAT. Okay. Okay.

Why did you tell me?

CATHERINE. What?

KAT. You contacted me. You told me what you were going to do today.

CATHERINE. I wanted you to know.

KAT. You wanted me to stop you.

CATHERINE. No.

KAT. You wouldn't have told anyone if you didn't think they might stop you.

CATHERINE. I wanted you to know that what you did. All those years ago. It wasn't for nothing. That's all.

KAT. Of course it was. No one noticed.

CATHERINE. They'll notice his time.
Everyone's gonna be talking about it.

Look at all these people. Soon as I go up they'll be filming every second.

No one's gonna miss me doing this.

KAT. Even if that's true.
It won't change anything

You want to know what it feels like?

Agony. The worst pain. You can't imagine.

CATHERINE. That's not gonna work.

KAT. No one wants you to do this.

CATHERINE. Are you joking? Look around you. The world is crying out for someone to do this.

She raises the lighter.

KAT. Wait! Your family.

The people who care about you.

Think how they'll feel.

You don't –

CATHERINE. I don't.

KAT. You don't want to die.
Fight it.
It's not too late.

Put the lighter down. Go home. Have a bath. Eat a lasagne.

What I did.

I had my reasons.

I'd almost forgotten. But I had some really good reasons. And they haven't gone away.

But god. It wasn't worth it. There is no cause in the world that is worth doing this Catherine, I promise you.

CATHERINE. You don't really believe that, do you?

KAT. Look at me. Years I've lived in pain. Can't breathe properly. Can't move properly. Skin too tight. It wasn't worth it. I didn't change a thing that day.

CATHERINE. That's not true.

You changed me. Seeing you do that. It changed me.

KAT. One person.
One person by themselves is –

CATHERINE. Maybe that's all it takes.

Because I'm here now doing this and maybe me doing this is the thing that will change the world.

Or maybe I'll just change one of those people watching. Change that girl, that man, that woman and maybe they'll be the ones who change the world.

Maybe if I do this my face will go around my name will ring out and people will see that if they don't like what's going on they can get up out of their chairs and do something about it. They'll see me on fire and think to themselves 'if that woman can do that then I can do something to stop the rot. I can do something to stop the rot.'

Maybe a hundred more will set themselves on fire, person after person after person going up in flames until the world gets better until the world gets better. Imagine that.

Or maybe not.

But I've got to try, right? Because we've tried everything else.

KAT. You can still go home.

CATHERINE. Is that what you want?

KAT. Of course.

CATHERINE. If I do this. What you did. All those years of pain. It could mean something. Don't you want that?

It's alright Kat. I'm ready.

It's nice. How calm I feel.

She raises the lighter.

KAT. There's a lot of good in this world.

CATHERINE. You're right. There is.

That's why we've got to fight for it.

What do you think? Should I do it?

KAT. I

CATHERINE. Should I do it?

It's alright. Don't worry. I'm okay.

Just say yes.

Ages.

And then.

KAT. Yes.

CATHERINE *smiles as she flicks the lighter.*

She's on fire.

So bright.

KAT *shields her eyes from the light.*

1

2

3

4

5

6

7

8

9

10

11

12

13

14

15

– The world gets… –

Other Titles in this Series

Mike Bartlett
ALBION
BULL
GAME
AN INTERVENTION
KING CHARLES III
WILD

Tom Basden
THE CROCODILE
HOLES
JOSEPH K
THERE IS A WAR

Deborah Bruce
THE DISTANCE
GODCHILD
THE HOUSE THEY GREW UP IN
SAME

Jez Butterworth
THE FERRYMAN
JERUSALEM
JEZ BUTTERWORTH PLAYS: ONE
MOJO
THE NIGHT HERON
PARLOUR SONG
THE RIVER
THE WINTERLING

Phil Davies
FIREBIRD

Vivienne Franzmann
BODIES
MOGADISHU
PESTS
THE WITNESS

James Fritz
COMMENT IS FREE
    & START SWIMMING
THE FALL
ROSS & RACHEL

Stacey Gregg
LAGAN
OVERRIDE
PERVE
SCORCH
SHIBBOLETH
WHEN COWS GO BOOM

Sam Holcroft
COCKROACH
DANCING BEARS
EDGAR & ANNABEL
PINK
RULES FOR LIVING
THE WARDROBE
WHILE YOU LIE

Vicky Jones
THE ONE
TOUCHED

Anna Jordan
CHICKEN SHOP
FREAK
YEN

Lucy Kirkwood
BEAUTY AND THE BEAST
    with Katie Mitchell
BLOODY WIMMIN
THE CHILDREN
CHIMERICA
HEDDA *after* Ibsen
IT FELT EMPTY WHEN THE
    HEART WENT AT FIRST BUT
    IT IS ALRIGHT NOW
LUCY KIRKWOOD PLAYS: ONE
MOSQUITOES
NSFW
TINDERBOX

Laura Lomas
BIRD & OTHER MONOLOGUES FOR
    YOUNG WOMEN

Ben Musgrave
CRUSHED SHELLS AND MUD
PRETEND YOU HAVE BIG
    BUILDINGS

Evan Placey
CONSENSUAL
GIRLS LIKE THAT
GIRLS LIKE THAT & OTHER PLAYS
    FOR TEENAGERS
PRONOUN

James Rushbrooke
TOMCAT

Stef Smith
GIRL IN THE MACHINE
HUMAN ANIMALS
REMOTE
SWALLOW

Jack Thorne
2ND MAY 1997
BUNNY
BURYING YOUR BROTHER IN
    THE PAVEMENT
HOPE
JACK THORNE PLAYS: ONE
JUNKYARD
LET THE RIGHT ONE IN
    after John Ajvide Lindqvist
MYDIDAE
THE SOLID LIFE OF SUGAR WATER
STACY & FANNY AND FAGGOT
WHEN YOU CURE ME
WOYZECK *after* Büchner

Phoebe Waller-Bridge
FLEABAG

Tom Wells
BROKEN BISCUITS
FOLK
JUMPERS FOR GOALPOSTS
THE KITCHEN SINK
ME, AS A PENGUIN

Carly Wijs
US/THEM

'A great published script makes you understand what the play is, at its heart' *Slate Magazine*

Enjoyed this book? Choose from hundreds more classic and contemporary plays from Nick Hern Books, the UK's leading independent theatre publisher.

Our full range is available to browse online now, including:

Award-winning plays from leading contemporary dramatists, including *King Charles III* by Mike Bartlett, *Anne Boleyn* by Howard Brenton, *Jerusalem* by Jez Butterworth, *A Breakfast of Eels* by Robert Holman, *Chimerica* by Lucy Kirkwood, *The Night Alive* by Conor McPherson, *The James Plays* by Rona Munro, *Nell Gwynn* by Jessica Swale, and many more...

Ground-breaking drama from the most exciting up-and-coming playwrights, including Vivienne Franzmann, James Fritz, Ella Hickson, Anna Jordan, Jack Thorne, Phoebe Waller-Bridge, Tom Wells, and many more...

Twentieth-century classics, including *Cloud Nine* by Caryl Churchill, *Death and the Maiden* by Ariel Dorfman, *Pentecost* by David Edgar, *Angels in America* by Tony Kushner, *Long Day's Journey into Night* by Eugene O'Neill, *The Deep Blue Sea* by Terence Rattigan, *Machinal* by Sophie Treadwell, and many more...

Timeless masterpieces from playwrights throughout the ages, including Anton Chekhov, Euripides, Henrik Ibsen, Federico García Lorca, Christopher Marlowe, Molière, William Shakespeare, Richard Brinsley Sheridan, Oscar Wilde, and many more...

Every playscript is a world waiting to be explored. Find yours at **www.nickhernbooks.co.uk** – you'll receive a 20% discount, plus free UK postage & packaging for orders over £30.

'Publishing plays gives permanent form to an evanescent art, and allows many more people to have some kind of experience of a play than could ever see it in the theatre' *Nick Hern, publisher*

www.nickhernbooks.co.uk

A Nick Hern Book

Parliament Square first published in Great Britain as a paperback original in 2017 by Nick Hern Books Limited, The Glasshouse, 49a Goldhawk Road, London W12 8QP, in association with the Royal Exchange Theatre, Manchester, and the Bush Theatre, London

Parliament Square copyright © 2017 James Fritz

James Fritz has asserted his right to be identified as the author of this work

Designed and typeset by Nick Hern Books, London
Printed in Great Britain by Mimeo Ltd, Huntingdon, Cambridgeshire PE29 6XX

A CIP catalogue record for this book is available from the British Library

ISBN 978 1 84842 708 2

CAUTION   All rights whatsoever in this play are strictly reserved. Requests to reproduce the text in whole or in part should be addressed to the publisher.

Amateur Performing Rights   Applications for performance, including readings and excerpts, by amateurs in the English language should be addressed to the Performing Rights Manager, Nick Hern Books, The Glasshouse, 49a Goldhawk Road, London W12 8QP, *tel* +44 (0)20 8749 4953, *email* rights@nickhernbooks.co.uk, except as follows:

Australia: Dominie Drama, 8 Cross Street, Brookvale 2100, *tel* (2) 9938 8686, *fax* (2) 9938 8695, *email* drama@dominie.com.au

New Zealand: Play Bureau, PO Box 9013, St Clair, Dunedin 9047, *tel* (3) 455 9959, *email* info@playbureau.com

South Africa: DALRO (pty) Ltd, PO Box 31627, 2017 Braamfontein, *tel* (11) 712 8000, *fax* (11) 403 9094, *email* theatricals@dalro.co.za

United States and Canada: Berlin Associates, as below

Professional Performing Rights   Applications for performance by professionals in any medium and in any language throughout the world should be addressed to Berlin Associates, 7 Tyers Gate, London SE1 3HX, *fax* +44 (0)20 7632 5296, *email* agents@berlinassociates.com

No performance of any kind may be given unless a licence has been obtained. Applications should be made before rehearsals begin. Publication of this play does not necessarily indicate its availability for performance.

Woodland
CARBON
www.woodlandcarbon.co.uk
NICK HERN BOOKS
Printed on Carbon Captured paper

www.nickhernbooks.co.uk

facebook.com/nickhernbooks

twitter.com/nickhernbooks